# Foraging

# Foraging

Paul Chambers

REMEMBER WHEN

First published in Great Britain in 2010
and reprinted in 2012 by

REMEMBER WHEN
An imprint of
Pen & Sword Books Ltd
47 Church Street
Barnsley
South Yorkshire
S70 2AS



ISBN 978 1 84468 084 9



A CIP catalogue record for this book is
available from the British Library



Typeset in 10pt Palatino by Mac Style, Beverley, East Yorkshire
Printed and bound in India by Replika Press Pvt. Ltd.

Pen & Sword Books Ltd incorporates the Imprints of Pen & Sword Aviation,
Pen & Sword Family History, Pen & Sword Maritime, Pen & Sword Military,
Pen & Sword Discovery, Wharncliffe Local History, Wharncliffe True Crime,
Wharncliffe Transport, Pen & Sword Select, Pen & Sword Military Classics,
Pen & Sword Politics, Pen & Sword Archaeology, Pen & Sword Atlas,
Leo Cooper, The Praetorian Press, Remember When, Claymore Press,
Seaforth Publishing and Frontline Publishing

For a complete list of Pen & Sword titles please contact
PEN & SWORD BOOKS LIMITED
47 Church Street, Barnsley, South Yorkshire, S70 2AS, England
E-mail: enquiries@pen-and-sword.co.uk
Website: www.pen-and-sword.co.uk

# Contents

*Preface* 9

*An Introduction to Foraging* 14
Getting Started 14
Gathering Technique 16
Identifying Plants 17
Preparation and Preservation Technique 20
The Golden Rules of Foraging 24

*How to Use this Book* 25

**Chapter 1** Garden and Urban 27
Borage – *Borago officinalis* 29
Burdock – *Arctium lappa*; *A. minus* 31
Common Chickweed – *Stellaria media* 33
Coltsfoot – *Tussilago farfara* 34
Dandelion – *Taraxacum officinale* 36
Ground Elder – *Aegopodium podagraria* 37
Rosemary – *Rosmarinus officinalis* 39
Wall Pennywort – *Umbilicus rupestris* 40
Hairy Bittercress – *Cardamine hirsuta* 41
Ivy-leaved Toadflax – *Cymbalaria muralis* 43
Greater Plantain – *Plantago major* 44
Biting Stonecrop – *Sedum acre* 45
Rosebay Willowherb – *Chamerion (Epilobium) angustifolium* 47
Red and White Dead Nettles – *Lamium purpureum*; *L. album* 48
Stinging Nettle – *Urtica dioica*; *U. urens* 49
Lime Tree – *Tilia europaea*; *T. cordata* 52

**Chapter 2** Hedgerows and Meadows 53
Agrimony – *Agrimonia eupatoria* 55
Blackthorn – *Prunus spinosa* 56
Cleavers – *Galium aparine* 57

Common Sorrel – *Rumex acetosa* 60
Garlic Mustard – *Alliaria petiolata* 61
Ground Ivy – *Glechoma hederacea* 63
Hawthorn – *Crataegus monogyna* 64
Horseradish – *Armoracia rusticana* 66
Primrose – *Primula vulgaris* 68
Tansy – *Tanacetum vulgare* 69
Wild Hops – *Humulus lupulus* 71
Woodland (Wild) Strawberry – *Fragaria vesca* 73
Wintercress – *Barbarea vulgaris* 75
Cow Parsley – *Anthriscus sylvestris* 76
Three-Cornered Garlic – *Allium triquetrum* 77
Sweet Cicely – *Myrrhis odorata* 79
Bistort – *Persicaria bistorta* 80
Blackberries – *Rubus fructicosus* 81
Good King Henry – *Chenopodium bonus-henricus* 83
Fat Hen – *Chenopodium album* 84
Mugwort – *Artemisia vulgaris* 85
Medlar – *Mespilus germanica* 88
Silverweed – *Argentina anserina* 89

**Chapter 3** Woodlands and Forests 91
Common Ash Tree – *Fraxinus excelsior* 92
Beech Tree – *Fagus sylvatica* 95
Sweet Chestnut – *Castanea sativa* 96
Crab Apple – *Malus sylvestris* 97
Ramsons – *Allium ursinum* 100
Elder Tree – *Sambucus nigra* 101
Hazel Tree – *Corylus avellana* 104
Wood Avens – *Geum urbanum* 105
Juniper – *Juniperus communis* 107
Rowan – *Sorbus aucuparia* 108
English Oak – *Quercus robur* 109
Pignut – *Conopodium majus* 111
Sweet Woodruff – *Galium odoratum* 112
Common Hogweed – *Heracleum sphondylium* 113
Common Broom – *Cytisus scoparius* 115
Wild Cherry – *Prunus avium* 116
Wild Raspberry – *Rubus idaeus* 117
Black and Red Currants – *Ribes nigrum* and *R. rubrum* 119

**Chapter 4** Grasslands and Heath 121
Bilberry – *Vaccinium myrtillus* 121
Wild Chamomile – *Anthemis nobilis* 124
Red Clover – *Trifolium pratense* 125
Corn Salad – *Valerianella locusta* 127
Common Gorse – *Ulex europaeus* 128
Heather – *Calluna vulgaris* 129
Salad Burnet – *Sanguisorba minor* 131
Sow Thistle – *Sonchus oleraceus; S. asper* 132
Yarrow – *Achillea millefolium* 133
Wild Marjoram – *Origanum vulgare* 135
Wild Thyme – *Thymus polytrichus* 136
Wild Basil – *Clinopodium vulgare* 137
Cowberry – *Vaccinium vitis-idaea* 139
Crowberry – *Empetrum nigrum* 140
Common Poppy – *Papaver rhoeas* 141
Mint – *Mentha* spp. 144
Catmint – *Nepeta cataria* 145
Wild Parsnip – *Pastinaca sativa* 147

**Chapter 5** Wetlands and Streams 149
Bog Myrtle – *Myrica gale* 151
Lady's Smock – *Cardamine pratensis* 152
Meadowsweet – *Filipendula ulmaria* 153
Watercress – *Rorippa nasturtium-aquaticum* 154
Common Comfrey – *Symphytum officinale* 156
European Cranberry – *Vaccinium oxycoccus* 157

**Chapter 6** The Coastal Fringe 159
Alexanders – *Smyrnium olusatrum* 160
Black Mustard – *Brassica nigra* 161
Fennel – *Foeniculum vulgare* 163
Common Mallow – *Malva sylvestris* 164
Marsh Samphire – *Salicornia europaea* 165
Red Valerian – *Centranthus ruber* 167
Rock Samphire – *Crithmum maritimum* 168
Scurvygrass – *Cochlearia officinalis; C. danica* 169
Sea Beet – *Beta vulgaris* subsp. *maritima* 171
Sea Kale – *Crambe maritima* 172
Sea Purslane – *Atriplex portulacoides* 173
Wild Cabbage – *Brassica oleracea* 175
Sea Carrot/Wild Carrot – *Daucus carota* 177

**Chapter 7** Seaweeds 179
Carragheen – *Chondrus crispus* 181
Purple Laver – *Porphyra umbilicalis* 183
Dulse – *Palmaria palmata* 185
Sea Lettuce – *Ulva lactuca* 187

**Chapter 8** The Forager's Calendar 189

**Chapter 9** A Summary of Plants 195

*Bibliography* 206

*Acknowledgements* 208

# Preface

Foraging for edible wild plants is a fun and practical hobby that is ideally suited to the modern world. We are daily confronted with concerns about climate change, supermarket dominance, genetically-modified organisms and sustainability; at a stroke the art of foraging addresses all these issues. The wild plants of Britain are a low carbon, sustainable resource that require no packaging, no wasteful processing, no air miles and, most amazingly of all, they are free and they taste great! Perhaps this is why foraging has become one of the fastest growing countryside hobbies of recent years.

Foraging is, of course, simply a modern name for practical skills that were at one time widespread among the rural population. In prehistoric and medieval times foraging was used to supplement poor agricultural diets and to stock up the winter larder. It was also a medicinal necessity with much of the preliminary botanical studies being undertaken by apothecaries who were eager to describe the plants which formed the ingredients of their medicinal concoctions. However, one does not need to travel far back in time to understand the usefulness of foraging: the rationing of food in the 1940s and 50s saw people turn to the hedgerows in search of additional cooking ingredients while recent historical crises, such as the Potato Famine in Ireland, caused foraging to become a survival skill. Indeed, my own relatives once foraged for seaweed and hedgerow plants during the near starvation conditions brought about by the German occupation of Jersey during the Second World War.

These days farmed food is plentiful and foraging is no longer a matter of life and death, but there has been a remarkable upsurge in its practice during recent years. What should have caused such an interest in foraging for wild food is a matter of debate. Some think it might be because the modern world of supermarkets and instant meals has placed a wide gap between ourselves and the source of the food we eat and foraging helps us to bridge this. Others say that it is simply a reflection of our search for a simpler, less cluttered lifestyle. However, I suspect that there are dozens of reasons why people are learning to forage, not least of which is because it is engaging, healthy and great fun. Whatever the reason, foraging in the twenty-first century is an established hobby that engages hundreds of thousands of people to a greater or lesser degree.

My own interest in foraging arose from a pre-existing passion for natural history. Like many amateur naturalists, I was well acquainted with the British countryside and knew that some of its plants were edible but I had rarely bothered to test this. My experiments

*A selection of summer fruit.*

**Below and opposite:** *A refreshing cup of herbal tea.*

The forager's winter larder.

went little further than picking a few blackberries or making the odd batch of nettle soup. Then, several years ago, a friend took me foraging along the hedgerows and footpaths close to his house. We left before sunrise on a late summer's day and within an hour had gathered enough food to take home and prepare a hearty breakfast for our still slumbering families. My eyes were opened to the art of foraging and the satisfying feeling of accomplishment that it can produce.

I bought a book on the subject and began to forage for my own food. At the time I was living in London but this did not prove to be a problem as the canal banks, heaths and suburban woodlands proved to be a great source for edible plants. Later my wife and I moved to the Hertfordshire countryside whereupon my horizons were further broadened, as they have been ever since.

When I started foraging I was not the world's best botanist (I prefer to study invertebrates) but it proved to be the ideal excuse to become better acquainted with the flora of Britain. As my interest grew, so I learned to identify dozens of plant species that I had hitherto not even noticed. I soon realised that foraging is not just a means of obtaining free food but, if done sensitively and correctly, it is a fascinating and absorbing outdoor pastime which has much to offer the amateur naturalist.

As an amateur naturalist who became a forager (rather than vice versa), I am disappointed with some of the books that have been written about Britain's edible plants. I feel that while most of these publications write admirably on the culinary delights of individual plants, they have rather forgotten the context of their natural history. I also feel that some of the books are not well organised, the plant species being listed alphabetically or even randomly. This does not reflect the way in which I undertake my foraging expeditions, which tend to be organised around trips to a certain part of the countryside (e.g. a woodland or the coast).

I have tried to address these perceived shortcomings by writing a book which I hope will appeal to beginner to intermediate foragers, to naturalists and to natural historians. I have structured the chapters in this book around the various natural environments in which the forager is liable to want to search for food (e.g. the seashore, woodlands, etc.). I hope that associating the plants with their usual environment will make the process of searching for and identifying them easier. (I freely acknowledge that this structure is not perfect, and that there are some plants which could have been placed in more than one chapter, but I hope it will suit most people.)

I have always rather admired John Gerard's *Great Herball*, a botanical-cum-herbalist work that was first published in 1597 and which remains in print. Gerard's plant entries are well-structured so that the reader can at a glance gather information on each species' ecology, appearance, uses and virtues. I have tried to ape Gerard's style by structuring individual plant entries in this book to include a wealth of information concerning botany, occurrence and culinary potential as well as on their historical use and any modern scientific interest. It is my hope that each plant in this book has been thoroughly explored and researched from several different angles, but especially from historical, scientific and culinary points of view.

I have included around a hundred of what I think are the most widespread, accessible and interesting British edible plant species. This should be more than enough to kick-start an interest in foraging and those who wish to delve deeper should consider joining a local group where experienced members will be able to pass on specialist knowledge and skills. When it comes to dealing with these plants in the kitchen, I will freely admit that I am not the world's best cook and that I prefer my cuisine to be practical and simple. This is probably reflected in these pages, where I have dwelt more on the general uses of individual plants, rather than reproducing complicated recipes. (That said, I have included many recipes and especially those from historical domestic manuals, which demonstrate how some of these plants were prepared centuries ago.) Those that need additional recipes for specific plants should consider searching the Internet where there are many forums, websites and groups devoted to foraging in Britain and northern Europe.

The reader should note that this book covers only plants and seaweeds. Foraging for animals, such as shellfish, is not included and my general uncertainty with identifying fungi (I am colour-blind and rely heavily on the advice of friends when picking them) has led to their exclusion. (It goes without saying that when it comes to foraging for mushrooms, many species of which are toxic, you need to be very sure indeed of your identification.) This book has taken a long time to research and write and it has allowed me to revisit some plant species that I had not eaten for some years. I hope sincerely that you will find this guide to be a useful introduction to the world of foraging. *Bon appétit*!

# An Introduction to Foraging

Foraging is a healthy and satisfying hobby but before you head off into the countryside with secateurs and basket at the ready, there are a few facts, techniques and rules of which you should be aware. Much of what follows is really just a matter of common sense and consideration. Even so, do not be tempted to skip this chapter as there are some legal and some health and safety issues associated with the picking of wild plants, of which all foragers will need to be aware.

## Getting Started

A person's first few foraging experiences can be daunting. The British countryside is home to hundreds of plant species, many of which look similar to each other, a situation that can be dispiriting and lead to doubts over identification (see below for advice on identifying plants). Like most hobbies, practice will make perfect, and the more experience you have

*Foraging can be a fun family activity.*

with the countryside, the more confident you will become. However, there is always the risk that the novice forager will be disheartened and so I will recommend a few things that may help to build up confidence.

Firstly, check the forager's calendar at the end of this book. This will tell you what sorts of edible plants are likely to be found at the time of year that you are searching. Generally the worst time of year for foraging is the winter, when only a few hardy plants will be in a fit state to eat. The best time is the spring and early summer, for plants, and the late summer and autumn for fruits and nuts.

Secondly, start off by foraging for simple, obvious plants which can be turned into eye-catching food for your family or friends. Cooking with stinging nettles, blackberries, elderflowers, sea beet, etc. will impress others and will give you the confidence to look for other edible plants.

Thirdly, consider finding like-minded people in your area or taking a course in foraging. The latter operate all over Britain (check the Internet for your closest one or for local groups) and, if run correctly, will offer a quick introduction to the techniques and plant species. Always take along a camera and a notebook.

I also recommend trying to involve family and friends as most foraging expeditions can be combined with a decent walk or a day out. Talk to your friends and neighbours about foraging: you will probably be surprised just how many of them have some experience of it (even if it's just gathering blackberries or sweet chestnuts). As with all journeys, the first few steps are often the hardest, so get out there and give it a go!

*Cut plants. Do not rip or tear them.*

## Gathering Technique

At all times the forager's first duty is to the conservation of the local environment and not to the needs of their stomach. In this respect, you should not uproot wild plants (this is actually illegal on public land, see below) or entirely denude them of their leaves and flowers. The plants you harvest must be left with enough resources to reproduce, so take small amounts of leaves, shoots, etc., from several plants and do not repeatedly return to the same area. Be especially careful with flowers and only pick them in situations where they are plentiful (e.g. on elderflower trees or gorse bushes). Do not rip, snap or tug shoots, flowers or leaves: cut them with a knife or secateurs. Likewise, do not dislodge fruit and nuts with sticks and stones: pick what is within reach or gather windfalls. It is generally better to gather the youngest leaves, shoots and buds as they will be more tender and hold more flavour.

As an alternative to wild foraging, some people gather the seeds of their favourite plants and cultivate them in their gardens (again, do not denude a plant of all its seeds). This is an age-old historical practice and is how many wild plants came to be domesticated into modern vegetable patches. If you are scared of introducing fast-spreading 'edible weeds' into your garden then cultivate them in pots, to help prevent them from spreading. We have a small garden but in it are two large pottery pots in which grow a selection of wild herbs. We have also managed to grow wild fennel, biting stonecrop and mallow in one of our flowerbeds (we are close to the sea, so these plants survive well).

It should almost go without saying that you must not trespass and must not forage on wildlife reserves or sites of special scientific interest (SSSIs). Think also of your personal safety and do not place yourself in dangerous situations (e.g. climbing cliffs and trees, fording rivers, etc.). Follow the Countryside Code and leave no sign of your presence and take all litter home with you.

Be aware of the Wildlife and Countryside Act (1981) which makes it **illegal to dig up or uproot any wild plant** or to pick or otherwise interfere with a select number of named endangered species (see www.jncc.gov.uk). Please note that while several plants in this book possess edible roots, the Wildlife and Countryside Act makes it illegal to obtain these from wild plants, although they may come from plants on private property with the permission of the landowner.

In addition to the specific plants covered by the Wildlife and Countryside Act, the Joint Nature Conservancy Council (JNCC) has a longer 'Red List' of threatened British plants which contains some 1,756 species (see www.jncc.gov.uk). The JNCC Red List categorises plant species on a scale that goes from 'Extinct' to 'Least Concern'. Three of the plants listed in this book fall into the medium category of 'vulnerable': good king Henry (*Chenopodium bonus-henricus*); catmint (*Nepeta cataria*); and wild carrot (*Daucus carota*). These three plants are widespread and often common but there is a worry that numbers might be in decline. It is best to assume that all plant species are under threat and to treat them accordingly.

Before setting off on a foraging expedition, take some basic precautions. Check the weather forecast (and tide times, if going on the beach) and dress appropriately for the conditions, including footwear and headgear. Take a mobile phone with you (in case of emergency) and, if necessary, a map marked with public rights of way, a compass and/or GPS (some of these should be put inside a waterproof bag). If travelling by car, I also put a spare set of clothes, food and water in the boot in case I get soaked or muddy. If going out for a long time then take something to eat and drink with you and some basic first aid equipment.

You will need a suitable container in which to place your foraged plants. A basket is generally better and more convenient than a rucksack. Do not use plastic bags as these may spoil the plants, especially on a warm day. Be careful when handling a knife or secateurs and consider bringing some stout gardening gloves for general searching and for thorny plants, stinging nettles and those plants whose sap may aggravate the skin (these are mostly in the carrot family). A camera can be handy for recording locations and individual plants.

It is sad to have to mention the issue of pollution but in an industrialised, overcrowded region such as Europe, it is an ever-present problem. There are many potential sources of pollution but the chief ones to be aware of come from cars, animals and farms. Be very wary of foraging for plants alongside busy roads which may receive car fumes or oily run-off. Watch out for areas that are heavily frequented by dog walkers (look for dog dirt left by ignorant pet owners) or areas that have been used to graze livestock. Where possible try to forage for plants that grow at a height that is greater than a hound's cocked hind leg. Farmland may be an obvious place to forage, but aside from the issue of trespass, plants growing at the edge of a field or in a meadow may have been sprayed with pesticides or herbicides. Other potential pollution sources include old industrial sites whose soil might hold heavy metals, etc., and bodies of water which may receive pollution from farmland (e.g. slurry) or contain disease-bearing organisms. Use your common sense and do not eat any plants unless they have been thoroughly washed and/or cooked.

## Identifying Plants

Learning to identify plants by sight is a frustrating process. It is, however, a basic and essential skill that foragers must learn if they are to avoid eating something that might be unpalatable or even poisonous. Finding the correct name for a plant that you have found will be a tricky process at first, but once you have made a positive identification, the quicker and easier it will be the next time. There are a number of useful things you can do to help the process along and the first is to get a decent identification guide.

I am not a botanist and the illustrations given in this book, while useful, will not necessarily provide you with a secure identification: for this you will need a good guide to the plants and flowers of the British Isles. Fortunately most high street bookshops will stock several such guides and often at reasonable prices.

Choose your guide carefully. The best ones are those that offer clear illustrations of the plants' flowers and leaves and which contain good written descriptions. For the beginner I recommend Paul Sterry's *Collins Complete Guide to British Wild Flowers* (HarperCollins, 2006) but be aware that this is an introductory guide which does not cover trees. It is, however, comprehensive, user-friendly and hard-wearing, as are several other similar guides.

*Don't ignore signs!*

*Dress appropriately for the weather.*

*The needs of agriculture can conflict with the needs of the forager.*

*Old industrial sites may remain polluted for years afterwards.*

Most amateur guides rely heavily on the plant's flowers and fruits as a means of identification. In some instances, the forager will want to find a plant before it flowers, as several species taste better like this. This is admittedly problematic and when learning to forage it is unquestionably easier to wait for a plant to flower before trying to identify it. There is a recently published affordable guide that overcomes the flowering problem: it is *The Vegetative Key to the British Flora* (John Poland, 2009) which, while being an excellent book for the experienced naturalist, may be off-putting for the absolute beginner.

When confronted with a plant that needs a name, most people will initially flick through their guide looking at the pictures, trying to match an illustration with the specimen before them. This is a perfectly valid means of obtaining an identification, but if your book has a 'key' then you really should consider using this as it can save a lot of time. (A key is a sort of written flow chart of plant features that, if followed correctly, will help you identify a specimen.) Even if you find a picture that looks identical to your specimen, always read the description as many plants look similar to one another.

Check all your identifications very carefully indeed, especially with some species of the carrot family where confusion with the deadly hemlock plant is possible. If you are in any doubt then do not eat a plant. Look for further illustrations and descriptions on the Internet (but bear in mind that you will be relying on the identification skills of others). Consider photographing the plant and submitting it to an Internet newsgroup where experts may be able to help.

By far the easiest means of learning the names and habitats of plants is to be shown them by somebody who is more experienced than yourself. If you cannot beg a favour from a knowledgeable friend, then consider joining a local botany group (try your local museum or learned society) or booking yourself onto a foraging course (look on the Internet). I have a number of friends who are happy to look at plants I have gathered or photographed and who will indulge me on a country walk or two. When you do get a solid identification, make notes of some obvious features about the plant that will enable you to identify it again more quickly.

## Preparation and Preservation Technique

After a day's foraging you should deal with the leaves, shoots, etc., you have gathered immediately. Most plant products will need to be thoroughly washed before use (there are some exceptions). This will help remove foreign objects, such as insects and dirt, as well as any unwanted chemical residues or animal by-products. A generally good rule is to fill a bowl or sink with water and soak the plants for several minutes, stirring them periodically. After this they can be rinsed under a tap and shaken or patted dry. Shoots and roots may need peeling or scrubbing.

Berries, nuts and fruits will normally store for a few days or weeks in a cool place or fridge, as will some shoots and most roots if left unpeeled (but check them regularly!). However, leaves and flowers will start to dehydrate and wilt quite rapidly and so should be washed and prepared straight away. There are a number of standard techniques for preparing and preserving foraged food; these will be mentioned quite often in this book and so the basic methods are given below.

### *Drying*

Aromatic leaves and flowers, and especially those that may loosely be called herbs, can often be dried and stored for later use. Air-drying is the most efficient method of preserving leaves and may be achieved using short stems of the plant. Before drying, remove any diseased or imperfect leaves, then wash them under cold water or blanch them for just a few seconds in boiling water. Shake off any excess water and then pat dry. This is important as any excess moisture will encourage the growth of mould, any sign of which will render the entire stem inedible.

Gather together half a dozen stems into a bunch and tie them together at the base. Place this upside down inside either a muslin drying bag or a paper bag that has had a number of holes punched through it. Hang this in a warm, dry place, such as an airing cupboard, above an Aga stove, or on a radiator. Leave it for anywhere from one week to a month, depending on the nature of the plant and the drying environment.

The drying process is complete when the leaves and stems are entirely brittle and crack with bending. Remove the bunch from the bag and check for any signs of disease or mould (if present, discard the whole bunch). Then strip the leaves and place in an airtight container (you could also hang the bunches up around the kitchen for decoration but the flavour will not last as long).

A second method is oven-drying, which is suitable for flowers and leaves. This requires you to wash and dry as described above but then remove the leaves and flowers from the stem and place them on a baking tray. Put the tray in an oven on its lowest setting (around 50°C) and check periodically until the leaves/flowers are dry and brittle. This method is quicker but the results are less predictable and, in my view, less satisfying. Do not be tempted to use a microwave oven!

### *Blanching and Freezing*

A good many of the plants in this book can be stored in the deep freeze for several weeks or months. This is an easy and efficient means of storing fleshy-leaved vegetables, berries and some fruits. All the techniques below will allow the fruit and vegetables to be stored for at least six months. Be sure to defrost them thoroughly before use.

Larger vegetables will need to be washed and cut into convenient sections. They should be blanched by placing in rapidly boiling water for a few minutes then removed and put in a bowl of cold water and left to cool down. When the vegetables have completely cooled, take them out and shake off any excess water, patting dry if necessary. Place the vegetables in bags or sealable containers and label with the date. Place in the freezer.

Fruit and berries are seasonal and so are ideal candidates for freezing for later use. Only use ripe fruit which shows no sign of damage or disease and wash and dry them well beforehand. When it comes to small berries, such as blackberries and crowberries, it is possible to freeze them whole by placing the fruit on a baking tray in the freezer and leaving overnight. The next day the fruit can be removed, put into labelled bags and placed in the freezer.

For larger and fleshier fruits, such as medlar, crab apples, strawberries and cherries, it is better to stew them before freezing. This is achieved by peeling and (if necessary)

*Hemlock is highly poisonous but it resembles several edible species. Make sure you know what you're eating!*

*Drying leaves and flowers is a cheap and effective means of storage.*

chopping the fruit, weighing it and then placing it in a heavy pan with enough water to stop it sticking to the bottom (a few tablespoons should be enough but keep an eye on the consistency). Heat until boiling, and then add approximately 100g of sugar for every 500g of fruit. Simmer for several minutes or until the fruit is entirely soft and pulpy. Take off the heat and allow to cool. If desired, the pulp can be strained through a sieve or colander (to remove stones, stalks or foreign objects) or it could be puréed through a blender. Bag the pulp, label it and freeze.

### *Jams and Jellies*

Turning berries and fruits into jams and jellies is a major preoccupation for many foragers as this is an efficient and delicious means of preserving fruit. Jars of home-made jam also make excellent thank-you gifts or small Christmas presents for friends and relatives.

The key to successful jam-making is to use fruit that is in good condition and which is preferably not overripe. The jam-making technique is relatively simple and involves reducing the fruit to a pulp by cooking, then adding a sufficient quantity of sugar to preserve it. Obtaining a jelly requires that the cooked fruit be strained overnight through a straining bag (available from cook shops) and the resultant liquid then boiled with sugar. The techniques needed for individual fruits are described with the plant entries in

*Many foragers will spend their autumn months making jam.*

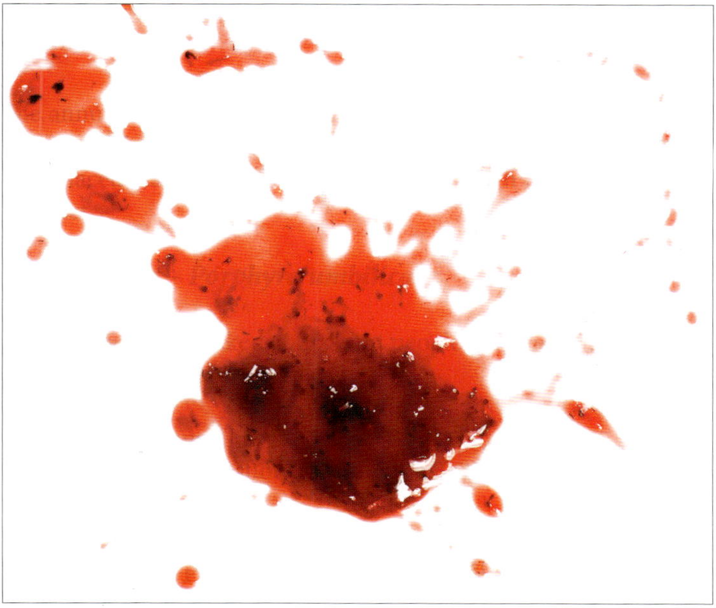

*Push your finger through a blob of jam to test for the setting point.*

the main section of this book. The trick is to add the correct amount of sugar and to know when the setting point has been reached (see below).

With regard to the amount of sugar, the ratios are given in the relevant entries but with some low-pectin fruit, such as blackberries, cherries, elderberries, strawberries and medlars, it may be better to use specialist jam-making sugar, which has extra pectin added to it. (Pectin is the compound which helps the jam or jelly to set.) Alternatively, add some lemon juice or lemon rind.

The setting point of the jam or jelly is reached at 104°C. This can be measured using a special jam thermometer (don't use a domestic thermometer!) or by periodic testing. To test for the setting point, put a small plate in the fridge and allow it to become cold. When you think you've reached the setting point, remove the plate from the fridge and drop onto it a small blob of the jam mixture. Push this gently with your finger: if the setting point has been reached then the top of the jam will wrinkle up. If you are unsure or if the wrinkling is not distinct, keep boiling and testing.

When the setting point has been reached, turn off the heat and ladle the mixture into clean, dry jars. If possible, sterilise the jars and dry in a low oven before use but often washing them in a dishwasher on a high temperature will suffice. After ladling the jam mixture into the jar, place a jam-maker's wax circle onto the top of the liquid; this prevents the growth of mould. Then seal the jar with a lid or plastic wrapper, label it and store in a dark, cool place for up to a year.

## The Golden Rules of Foraging

Below is a list of the golden rules that you should follow when foraging in the countryside. These are there to prevent unnecessary damage to the environment and for the safety of the individual forager. Most have been stated already in this chapter but they are important so I have repeated them in an easy-to-consult form:

- Do not forage on private land, wildlife reserves or Sites of Special Scientific Interest.
- Use a knife or secateurs to cut leaves, flowers and shoots. Do not strip individual plants of their leaves, shoots and especially their flowers. Forage from several plants and only pick what you need.
- Do not return to the same area again and again. Allow it to recover.
- Be aware of local pollution sources. If possible, pick away from busy roads, car parks and heavily cultivated land.
- Check your plant identification very carefully. Be aware of poisonous plants and of plants that may be endangered or subject to the Wildlife and Countryside Act. If in doubt, do not pick and do not eat.
- Do check the weather forecast, tide times and dress appropriately. Take a mobile phone with you and some basic safety equipment. If going to a new or remote area, take a map and navigational aids (compass or GPS).
- Do not leave litter, do shut gates behind you, obey notices, be wary of livestock and follow the Countryside Code!

# How to Use this Book

To forage successfully requires an understanding of the sorts of environment where edible plants might be expected to grow and the time of year when they will be found. When it comes to choosing a suitable place to grow, most plants are quite specific in their requirements and will only thrive if the climatic and soil conditions (among other things) are suited to their particular biology.

The British Isles have a temperate climate that is influenced by the Atlantic Ocean and consequently play host to a wide range of habitats, most of which will have their own unique plant species. I have structured this book so that each chapter deals with one broad habitat type from the British countryside. I believe that this reflects how most people undertake their foraging expeditions in that they will tend to go to a specific area, such as a wood, and spend some time searching there. I hope that grouping the plants by habitat will make the process of identification easier. The disadvantage of this is that some plant species may be found in more than one environment and thus should, by rights, appear in more than one chapter. I have therefore placed each plant in the habitat chapter that reflects where it is most likely to be found.

The other major factor that controls the occurrence of individual plants is the seasonality of the climate. Different seasons will bring forth different plants and will dictate which parts of a plant may be eaten. Those who need to know the best time of year to search for particular plants should consult the forager's calendar at the end of this book.

A major part of this book consists of individual edible plant species, each of which has an entry devoted to it. I have tried to approach these entries from the viewpoint of a naturalist and natural historian as well as that of a forager. In this respect I have offered an introductory summary of each plant's botanical attributes, including its scientific name, common name, distribution and occurrence. Whenever possible I have included historical and local names and the plant's etymology.

There is a cookery section which details how to forage for the plant, how to prepare and how best to eat it. I am a naturalist more than I am a *cordon bleu* chef and so, rather than relying on dozens of complicated recipes of dubious worth, I have taken a general approach towards cooking these plants for the dinner table. Specific recipes are provided when they really enhance the flavour of the plant or require specialist techniques. I have also included some 'receipts' (as recipes were once called) from a number of historical domestic manuals; these are mostly for the sake of interest rather than being a recommended means of cooking.

In historical times many of the plants that are covered in this book were not gathered because of their culinary benefits, but instead because they were believed to possess certain medicinal properties that could help in the treatment of disease or injury. Indeed, some of the earliest botanical works produced in Britain were herbalist treatises designed to help apothecaries find the right plants to help treat their patients. This practice continued into the early nineteenth century but became less popular with the arrival of more formal pharmaceutical products (some of which were themselves derived from plants).

I have offered a summary of some of the medicinal properties afforded to individual plants in a separate section. This information has been gathered from a number of historical works, including the famous 'herbals' written by John Gerard and Nicholas Culpeper. However, it should be noted that I have attached **no scientific weight** to this information and I strongly recommend that readers do not use these historical observations to treat modern medical disorders. At best they might be ineffective; at worst they could exacerbate a medical situation. This herbalist information is presented purely for the sake of interest, nothing more.

As well as offering a historical perspective to the plants, I thought it would be interesting to see what the scientific community has had to say about various plant species. Using specialist databases available in some London libraries, I looked at what has been written in the scientific press (and especially peer-reviewed journals) about the plant species covered by this book. In some instances very little has been written but others had some surprising results. I offer a brief summary of the interesting things that have been discovered about each plant, especially in relation to any medicinal or pharmaceutical studies. Again, I do not place any reliance on these notes. Many are based on laboratory studies rather than clinical trials, with the results being merely suggestive of a plant's potential, rather than an endorsement of it as a treatment for a specific medical disorder. We are still a long way from discovering the full pharmaceutical potential that doubtless lies within Britain's diverse flora, so for the time being we must be content with enjoying the plants for their beauty and edible qualities.

## *Chapter One*

# Garden and Urban

An early introduction to the wonders of foraging came about in my back garden. It was a warm summer's day and I was relaxing around a BBQ with friends when one of them remarked that there were three edible plants growing within a few feet of where we sat. These turned out to be hairy bittercress and dandelions, which were growing on the lawn, and a profusion of garlic mustard which had established itself in a neglected flowerbed. Based on my friend's advice, we added some of the leaves to our salad bowl. All agreed that the bittercress and dandelions were delicious but not everyone was convinced by the garlic mustard, it holding a somewhat unusual taste. This was an eye-opening moment which encouraged an interest in edible plants. Naturally enough, the first place I started to look was in my own backyard.

*A green corridor in the city.*

Foraging in gardens, parks and metropolitan sites can be very rewarding, not least because it will probably introduce you to the wonders of urban wildlife. It is usual to think of our crowded, sprawling towns and city centres as being the antithesis of Nature but there is always space enough for plants and wild flowers to thrive. There are, for example, gardens, parks, canal banks, commons, playing fields, allotments and unused railway cuttings (be wary of abandoned railway tracks as these may be polluted, see below). Some plants just need the smallest patch of soil and access to a modicum of sunlight and rain. Even the cracks in walls and pavements will play host to species of tenacious plants whose roots can exploit the thin soil that accumulates within.

The selective nature of human aesthetics means that many of the edible plants listed in this section are often labelled as weeds and so are uprooted and destroyed at the gardener's earliest convenience. For this reason well-manicured gardens are usually not the best to forage. Instead try looking in neglected gardens, round the edge of allotments or in urban spaces that have been deliberately left to grow wild (e.g. commons, heaths or the wilder parts of some parks and playing fields). When living in London I would look along the canal towpaths, in parks or travel to some of the larger open spaces such as Hampstead Heath or Epping Forest. There is always somewhere where wild plants will thrive in sufficient quantity to allow the forager to do their thing.

An alternative to urban foraging is to give over a part of your garden or allotment to wild flowers. Often 'weeds' such as cleavers, garlic mustard, nettles and plantains will be the first to colonise barren ground, so digging an area over at the end of winter and leaving it should ensure that some edible plants will make their presence known. Other edible plants can be deliberately sown by gathering their seeds (be sparing when taking seeds from wild plants) and sowing them in the garden.

Urban foraging brings with it a heightened risk of inadvertent trespassing and pollution. Always follow the golden rules of foraging: do not be tempted to trespass; search carefully and considerately, being careful not to damage or disorganise property or ornamental plants. Urban pollution may come in several forms but most notably from the application of toxic herbicides or pesticides to control the spread of plants and insects (e.g. glycophosphate) and from heavy metals and other potential toxins residing in the soil. It is difficult to see at a glance which areas may be affected, but in general terms one should avoid manicured gardens and parks (where herbicides might have been used). Similarly, avoid old industrial sites, railway tracks, etc., where the ground may have been subjected to the by-products of manufacturing or heavy machinery. Those who are worried about industrial pollution in an area could look through historical maps at a local library as these will reveal what was on a site in years gone by. Check the soil for industrial litter such as screws, nails, plastics, clinker and oil. Some plants will adsorb toxins more readily than others (e.g. brassicas) and if in any doubt of an area's suitability, then do not forage there. Other problems include animal faeces (dogs, cats, rats and humans), physical hazards such as broken glass and heavy masonry, and officious residents who may object to you foraging close to their house.

## Borage – *Borago officinalis*

> 'The leaves and roots are to very good purpose used in putrid and pestilential fevers…'
>
> Nicholas Culpeper, 1652

- Alternative Name: Starflower
- Etymology: Celtic *borrach*, a noble person
- Annual; generally gardens but sometimes in waste ground. England, Wales and southern Scotland. It has blue flowers, oval leaves and is very bristly.

Borage is a sturdy, hairy herb plant of Middle Eastern origin which was imported and cultivated in Asian and European gardens for use in cookery and medicine. The ancient Romans were fond of it and, according to Pliny, called it *buglossus*, which is Greek for 'ox tongue', because of the shape of its leaves. At other times it was known as *euphrasynon* (from the Greek/Latin for 'gladness') because of its alleged ability to enhance the happiness of a drunken crowd when added to their wine.

Borage leaves have a mild but refreshing cucumber-like taste and may be picked during the spring and summer; the distinctive blue, star-shaped flowers are also edible and have a sweet taste. They may be gathered from mid-spring to early summer.

*Cookery:* Although popular in historical times, both in culinary and medicinal terms, by the early nineteenth century borage had fallen out of general use. It was, according to the Georgian gardener Philip Miller, seldom used except 'to make cool tankards which are a pleasant and wholesome summer drink'.

The use of borage to flavour cool drinks led to its inclusion in the original version of Pimms, an alcoholic drink that was created in the 1820s by the Londoner James Pimm (it was later replaced by mint). In continental Europe borage is still used as an ingredient in pickles, soups and salads.

Borage leaves may be picked, washed and used raw as an addition to salads or as a garnish for soups and light pasta dishes. The flowers have been used to add an attractive garnish to a variety of cold desserts, such as ice cream and fruit fools. Borage is one of the ingredients of 'green sauce', a mayonnaise-like concoction eaten in Germany, France, Italy and Spain which contains the leaves of several herbs.

*BORAGE SUMMER DRINK (based on an 1803 recipe)*
Place into a blender a generous sprig of borage, one peeled and diced cucumber and the juice of two limes or a quantity of lime cordial. Add approximately 0.8 litre of water and four tablespoons of sugar. Blend then sieve into a jug and add ice (dilute if too strong; add more sugar if not sweet enough).

*Borage (p. 29).*

*Historical Uses:* During medieval times the alleged ability of borage to induce happiness led to its being grown extensively as a medicinal plant. In the early seventeenth century Francis Bacon noted that 'the leaf of the borage hath an excellent spirit, to repress the fuliginous vapour of dusky melancholy, and so to cure madness'. This viewpoint is represented in folklore by the motto, 'with borage comes courage', and by the Elizabethan herbalist Gerard's belief that borage would comfort the heart, drain away sorrow and 'purgeth melancholie'.

Historical herbalists recommend that borage leaves are best used when fresh and that they should not be dried (although they can be distilled or boiled up into a syrup, jars of which would be found in many apothecary stores).

*Scientific Notes:* Borage is part of the Boraginaceae family and as such is related to comfrey and forget-me-nots. Borage seed oil (also called starflower oil) may be found in health food shops where it is marketed as a dietary supplement. It is rich in gamma-linolenic acid, palmitic acid, stearic acid, oleic acid, linoleic acid, eicosenoic acid, erucic acid and nervonic acid. The dietary benefit of borage is untested but a clinical trial published in 2005 did suggest that the administration of gamma-linolenic acid derived from borage oil could lessen the effects of an alcohol-derived hangover. Borage seed oil has anticoagulant properties and is not recommended for those taking blood-thinning drugs such as Warfarin.

*Burdock.*

## Burdock – *Arctium lappa; A. minus*

> 'The roots have a sweetish taste at first, followed by a slight austerity and bitterness.'
> Benjamin Barton, 1837

- Alternative Names: Bur, Clot Bur
- Etymology: Greek *arktos*, a bear, from the roughness of its burrs
- Biennial; waste ground and hedgerows; *A. minus* occurs across much of Britain while *A. lappa* has a more southerly distribution. It has purple flowers and large heart-shaped leaves.

This common plant grows readily on waste ground as well as in neglected gardens and by roadsides. It is familiar because of the mass of sticky burrs that are eagerly stripped by schoolchildren and then hurled at their colleagues, the hope being that they will cling to their clothes. Similarly, the burrs will frequently turn up in the shaggy coats of dogs, cats and sheep. In times past children would allegedly throw the burrs at bats' wings as this was said to cause them to fall to the ground.

The stems and roots are edible (see Introduction regarding the uprooting of wild plants) and have an earthy taste that reminds me of celery but which is more usually compared to that of the artichoke (the root is more bitter than the stems). It may be foraged for during late spring and summer.

*Cookery:* Modern British cuisine does not utilise burdock other than as a flavouring in 'dandelion and burdock', a soft, naturally effervescent drink which dates to medieval times and is alleged to increase milk yield in breast-feeding mothers. Dandelion and burdock is readily available on supermarket shelves but many mass-produced cordials and canned drinks contain, or are enhanced with, artificial flavourings rather than using extracts from the plant. Other than this, burdock is only widely eaten in eastern Asia and especially Japan.

There are two parts of the burdock plant which are edible. The first is the young stems which should be picked before the flowers arrive and stripped of their bark. In historical times these would be boiled or eaten raw like asparagus with oil and vinegar, but they can be added to salads and are deep-fried in Italy to produce 'battered frittata'. The second, more common, edible part is the taproots which are thin, wiry and may extend for some distance underground (see Introduction regarding the uprooting of wild plants). These roots, when cleaned, have quite a harsh taste and may be dried and then powdered in a spice grinder. Alternatively, the roots may be shredded, soaked in water and then used in stir-fries in conjunction with other crisp vegetables such as carrots.

*DANDELION AND BURDOCK DRINK*

Take one large saucepan with 600ml of boiling water and add one and a half teaspoons each of powdered dandelion and burdock root. (Raw roots, two for each plant, may be used but should be chopped roughly and boiled for half an hour before adding other ingredients.) Take a thumb-sized piece of fresh ginger and finely chop; add this to the water with a teaspoon of lemon juice. Simmer the mixture for 20–30 mins, then filter through a straining bag or very fine sieve. Add 300g of sugar and stir until dissolved (if necessary put on a gentle heat), then dilute with cold water/sparkling water/lemonade at a ratio of around one part mixture to four parts water. This should make a refreshing summer drink.

*Historical Uses:* Burdock was not a well-liked plant in times gone by and was considered by most to be a weed. 'Few quadrupeds, except the ass, will touch this plant,' muttered one Victorian gardener although an earlier authority, Dr Jonathan Stokes, noted that 'a horse eats the burrs; birds eat the seeds; and snails and caterpillars eat the leaves'. At one time it did have a place in some medicinal gardens as an herb that could be used to detoxify the body and purify the blood, although most physicians preferred to use sarsaparilla for this task. One old herbalist recipe recommends adding dried burdock roots to three pints of boiling water then evaporating this down to two pints. The ill patient was then given a pint of the strained juice each day until they recovered.

*Scientific Notes:* Burdock is in the Asteraceae family of plants and is related to the daisies and thistles. In recent times extracts of burdock root oil have found their way into a variety of hair care products such as shampoos and conditioners. This is because of its alleged ability to strengthen hair, promote its growth and to effect a cure for a variety of skin complaints such as dandruff and psoriasis. Burdock root is also an ingredient in essiac tea which is claimed to have immune-enhancing and disease-fighting properties. However, the only proven medicinal property of essaic tea is that it is a laxative. Burdock is generally high in fibre and amino acids.

## Common Chickweed – *Stellaria media*

> 'It is a fine, soft, pleasing herb under the dominion of the moon.'
>
> Nicholas Culpeper, 1652

- Alternative Names: Winterweed, Chickenwort
- Etymology: Latin, *stella*, a star, from the shape of its flower
- Annual; generally on waste ground across all Britain. It has white flowers, ovate leaves and a hairy line down the stem.

There are several British species of chickweed but here we are dealing with the commonest which may frequently be found as a garden weed. It produces small white flowers and may spread across open ground quickly. Traditionally the flowers have been used as a makeshift barometer: when they are open the weather will be fine but if they are closed then 'let the traveller put on his great coat'. Chickweed also exhibits what used to be called 'the sleep of plants', which means that at night its leaves move to cover up the plants' tender shoots.

Chickweed is said to get its name because birds, including young chickens, are fond of eating it, and it was at one time fed to songbirds. It is a classic green vegetable with a taste that may be compared with that of spinach. The leaves and flowers may be picked and eaten in the spring and autumn.

*Cookery:* There are few acknowledged uses for chickweed in British or European cookery, although there is an eighteenth-century reference to 'its tender shoots and leaves, when boiled, being scarcely distinguished from early spinach, and are in every respect as wholesome'.

In modern cookery chickweed leaves should be picked with scissors during the spring and autumn, when the plant is fresh and succulent. It is best eaten raw and should be thoroughly washed for use in salads (add one or two handfuls). The leaves also taste great when added into light vegetable or chicken soups; add a handful or so at the early stage of cooking. The chopped leaves may also be added to Mediterranean dishes such as risotto and pasta.

*Historical Uses:* Chickweed has been afforded a number of medicinal qualities. When boiled with pig's grease it is said to calm convulsive children, while its juice was used to treat painful ears, itching eyes, ulcers, liver complaints, cramps and scabs. Modern herbalists have been known to prescribe chickweed for skin complaints and joint pains.

*Chickweed flowers (p. 33).*

*Scientific Notes:* Chickweed is one of the few commonly foraged plants within the family Caryophyllaceae (sometimes called the 'pink family') of flowers which includes the campion and pearlwort species. The traditional medicinal properties afforded to chickweed do not seem to have been assessed scientifically.

## Coltsfoot – *Tussilago farfara*

'Coltsfoot is not altogether a useless plant.'

Robert Mudie, 1837

- Etymology: Greek, *tussis*, a cough, related to a medicinal use for the plant
- Perennial; waste ground and gardens across all Britain. It has yellow flowers and angular leaves which have a downy texture underneath.

According to herbalists, coltsfoot could be used to help with lung complaints and especially chesty coughs. It was also widely smoked as a mild tobacco ('northern tobacco' because the practice was prevalent in the north of England) which probably did nothing to help the lungs. The practice of smoking coltsfoot has recently been revived in some parts of Europe where smoking bans have been enacted in public places. One British

Coltsfoot.

confectionery firm sells 'coltsfoot rock', a hard sweet which incorporates the plant and whose taste is unusual but not unpleasant.

In my opinion (which I know is shared by some other foragers) coltsfoot tastes far too bitter to be considered truly edible. The plant is rarely gathered for food and its main use focuses on spring flowers which can be utilised in brewing wine and beer.

*Cookery:* There is little historical mention of coltsfoot being used as a cookery ingredient, and its main use was as an ingredient for use in brewing ale and wine. In such an instance a large quantity of flowers would be picked in spring and then added wholesale at the start of the brewing/fermenting process. In other respects I must agree with the Victorian author who noted that coltsfoot 'is inodorous, mucilaginous, rather disagreeably bitter and styptic to the taste'.

*Historical Uses:* For centuries coltsfoot has been used extensively to help in the relief of lung complaints such as colds, asthma and tuberculosis but the raw leaves are also suggested to help with burns and swellings, as well as 'disorders of the private parts'. In most instances the remedy is offered as a juice made from boiling up the leaves, then adding sugar or honey and reducing the mixture. Even in the modern day it is possible to buy 'coltsfoot rock', a medicinal sweet that is exclusively manufactured by the British company Stockley's Sweets. Below is an herbalist recipe from 1739 but, given its unusual ingredients, I do not recommend it to the reader:

> 'TAKE earthworms, well-warmed, a pound; snails (with shells on), well bruised, a gallon; coltsfoot (six ounces); maidenhair (two ounces); ground ivy; liverwort; hart's-tongue; and Egrimony. Infuse all these in three gallons of milk all night. The next day distil it, and take a glass every morning and afternoon.'

*Scientific Notes:* Coltsfoot is part of the daisy family (Asteraceae). There has been little research into the medical properties of chickweed extracts but it has been suggested that excessive consumption of the plant might lead to liver problems.

## Dandelion – *Taraxacum officinale*

> 'Boys may then be seen blowing off the feathery fruit, when ripe, to find out "what's o'clock".'
>
> Benjamin Barton, 1837

- Alternative Name: Monk's Head
- Etymology: Greek, *tarasso*, to change, from its effect on the blood
- Perennial; abundant in gardens and uncultivated ground across Britain. It has a distinctive yellow flower and serrated leaves that grow outwards from the root.

'A college youth that flashes for a day,' wrote the eighteenth-century poet James Hurdis of the dandelion, referring to its short-lived bright yellow flower. The common dandelion is surely one of our most widespread and recognisable plants. Its colourful flowers and wispy, globular seed-heads attract the attention of children, while the attentive gardener will spend many hours per year digging up and removing these weeds from their lawns and flower-beds.

Dandelion has much the same taste as many green vegetables but with a slightly bitter bite to it. The plant may be eaten all year round but tastes best when gathered during the spring.

*Cookery:* The dandelion (whose name is said to come from the French *dent de lion* – 'lion's tooth') has been widely used as a food. There are instances of it having been grown indoors during the winter so that its leaves could be used as a substitute for lettuce and, of course, there is the traditional drink 'dandelion and burdock' which may still be found in shops today (see entry for BURDOCK). It has also at times been used as a substitute for coffee and in historical times the French are said to have eaten the young roots and leaves on bread and butter (see Introduction regarding the uprooting of wild plants).

Generally the main edible parts of the plant are its roots, leaves and flowers which may be consumed raw or blanched. They should ideally be gathered in the spring when the plant is rejuvenating but the plant may be eaten all year round. After washing, the various parts of the plant may be added raw into salads, soups and broths.

Below is a historical recipe for dandelion coffee which, if done correctly, bears a vague resemblance to chicory coffee but will perhaps be too bitter for the modern palate.

*DANDELION COFFEE (1830 recipe)*
Dig up the roots of dandelion, wash them well, but do not scrape them; dry them, cut them in bits the size of peas, and then roast them in an earthen pot or coffee-roaster of any kind, and grind them in the coffee-mill, or bruise them in any way. The great secret of good coffee is to have it fresh-burnt and fresh-ground.

*Historical Uses:* Raw dandelion leaves were believed to have general health-giving properties, while the juice from boiled dandelion roots and leaves was said to be a diuretic and to relieve colds and fevers. An 1828 medical journal speaks of its ability to cure indigestion and other complaints: 'I have seen the patient restored by a strong decoction of dandelion, without the aid of other medicine. In addition to its effect on the liver, it tends to cool, and, consequently, allay the inflammatory diathesis, and, often, it excites both the bowels and the kidneys.'

*Scientific Notes:* The common dandelion is a member of the daisy family (Asteraceae) of flowering plants. All dandelions are high in potassium and there have been fears expressed that gross consumption of the plant or its extracts could lead to excessive levels of this compound occurring in the blood.

## Ground Elder – *Aegopodium podagraria*

'The Aegopodium has an acrid, pungent root.'

James Smith, 1803

- Alternative Names: Goutweed, Ashweed, Herb Gerard
- Etymology: Greek, *aigos*, a goat and *pous*, a foot; from the shape of its leaves
- Perennial; damp waste ground across all of Britain. It has white flowers, ovate leaflets and a grooved, hollow stem.

Ground elder is a widespread plant that may be found in a variety of situations including hedgerows, waste ground and gardens where, once established, it is difficult to remove, making it something of a menace to horticulturalists. The plant is aromatic with a spiky, peppery taste that will probably not be to everyone's liking. Ground elder should be foraged for its tender leaves and shoots during the springtime. WARNING: ground elder resembles the highly poisonous plant hemlock (*Conium maculatum*). Check your identification carefully and if in any doubt, do not eat.

Dandelion (p. 36).

Ground elder (p. 37).

Rosemary (opposite).

*Cookery:* In historical Sweden ground elder would be boiled up to be eaten as a side vegetable in the same manner as spinach or cabbage. The best means I have found of cooking it is to take a handful of the leaves and shoots and steam them lightly before serving with butter or garlic butter. This makes a good alternative to the more usual greens (such as spinach) but the strong, sometimes pungent, flavour means that it will not suit the taste of all diners. It may also be used as a minor ingredient in other dishes such as vegetable soups, pasta and omelettes.

*Historical Uses:* In historical times ground elder was often referred to as 'goutweed' because of its apparent ability to relieve the symptoms of this disease as well as the symptoms of arthritis and sciatica. To achieve this, the young buds and roots would either be boiled up and eaten or, in the case of pain relief, placed on the afflicted part of the body. Its use for such was expounded in the sixteenth and seventeenth centuries, but by the late eighteenth century its curative properties were dismissed by several medical authorities. One herbalist considered the plant to be 'possessed of nutrient rather than medicinal properties' while another stated that it 'has no right as to its name of goutweed'.

*Scientific Notes:* Ground elder is part of the carrot family (Apiaceae) of plants which includes many edible plants as well as some poisonous ones (e.g. hemlock). The plant has not been studied for its medical benefits but extracted lectin compounds from this, and related plants, are currently being assessed for their biological effect on cells.

## Rosemary – *Rosmarinus officinalis*

> 'Rosemary has an agreeable odour, and a warm pungent taste, nearly resembling lavender.'
>
> George Spratt, 1829

- Etymology: Latin, *rosmarinus*, old name for this plant
- Evergreen; not wild but found cultivated in many situations. It is fragrant with flowers that may be white, pink, purple or blue.

Rosemary is a familiar ornamental plant in flower-beds, parks and urban places. It is not a native British species but comes originally from southern Europe. However, the plant tolerates Britain's climate well, especially when tended to in domestic or ornamental gardens. The narrow spiky leaves have a strongly aromatic flavour and distinctive smell (reminiscent of pine needles); the plant is a well-known herb that has been used for decades to enhance roast meat dishes and bread.

*Cookery:* Rosemary leaves may be picked at any time of the year and used either fresh or dried and stored. In my experience it is best used in its most traditional form, as an addition to roast meat dishes when sprigs of the plant may be placed in the roasting tin or small bunches of leaves inserted into cuts in the meat. For rosemary bread, take a handful of leaves, mash them up with olive oil (and garlic, if desired), then rub them across the risen, shaped, bread dough and bake in the oven as usual.

*Historical Uses:* Rosemary was well-known to historical apothecaries, it probably having been introduced to Britain by the Romans. Among the many ascribed medical properties are as a curative for head colds, baldness, gout, bad memory and asthma. Its distinctive smell has led to the herb being used in potpourri and it may currently be found as a perfume ingredient within essential oils, shampoos and soaps. Modern herbalist uses include its prescription as a mild anti-depressant.

*Scientific Notes:* Rosemary belongs to the dead-nettle family (Lamiaceae) of plants. Recent laboratory trials suggest that rosemary may have anti-depressant and anti-inflammatory properties but these have yet to be tested on human subjects. Rosemary oil is believed to have anti-fungal qualities and has been tested as a possible inhibitor to the growth of certain toxic moulds.

## Wall Pennywort – *Umbilicus rupestris*

> 'The juice or the distilled water being drank, is very effectual for to cool a fainting hot stomach, a hot liver, or the bowels.'
>
> Nicholas Culpeper, 1652

- Alternative Names: Navelwort, Pennypies, Wall Pennyroyal, Kidney Wort
- Etymology: Latin, *umbilicus*, the navel, from the shape of the leaves
- Perennial; damp walls and banks in western parts of Britain. It has circular, fleshy leaves with a tall spike of pinkish flowers.

Wall pennywort may be found growing within the cracks and joints of stone walls or on steep earth banks in the shaded parts of woodlands. In the right conditions wall pennywort can grow in great profusion but in some areas the plant is considered to be rare, in which instance it should be left alone. The fleshy leaves have a fresh, bitter taste that is ideally suited to salads and garnishes. They are best picked during the spring and summer, although in some temperate areas the plant may survive throughout the year.

*Cookery:* It is the fleshy, broad circular leaves of the wall pennywort that should be picked and washed for eating raw; there are no traditional recipes which specifically utilise pennywort leaves but their crisp, succulent taste makes them an ideal addition to salads or as a garnish scattered across a cooked dish.

*Historical Uses:* The sixteenth-century herbalist John Gerard once complained that 'ignorant apothecaries' would confuse the medically beneficial wall pennywort with the 'extremely dangerous and destructive' marsh pennywort, sometimes at the cost of a patient's life. (Marsh pennywort is not to my knowledge poisonous, although Linnaeus claimed that it could be used to kill flies, but it grows only in wetland areas and so should not be eaten because of the risk of contracting waterborne parasites.) The medicinal properties afforded to the wall pennywort are remarkably few, it chiefly being described as having diuretic qualities, the ability to cool an overheated stomach, liver or kidney and as a dressing for bleeding wounds.

*Scientific Notes:* Wall pennywort is part of the stonecrop family (Crassulaceae). There have been no trials to test the medicinal or other properties of the wall pennywort.

## Hairy Bittercress – *Cardamine hirsuta*

'A pretty ornament to the sides of most meadows.'
Nicholas Culpeper, 1652

- Alternative Names: Shaggy Cuckoo-Flower, Hairy Ladies' Smock
- Etymology: Greek *kardia*, the heart, and *damao*, to fortify, from its medicinal properties.
- Annual; gardens and waste ground across all Britain. It has white flowers, each with four stamens.

Hairy bittercress is a widespread and hardy plant that will readily colonise bare ground and, although frequently admired as a wild flower, is considered to be an invasive weed by many gardeners. Referred to as 'lady-smocks' by Shakespeare, this plant would at one time colonise ploughed fields to such a degree that their mass of white flowers was said to look like linen that had been left out to dry in the sun. The leaves have a peppery taste in much the same way as watercress or rocket. They are best gathered and eaten during the spring.

*Cookery:* There is little historical reference to the use of hairy bittercress in traditional cookery, probably because the piquant taste it imparts may more easily be obtained from watercress and other supermarket plants. Hairy bittercress leaves may be picked during the spring, summer and autumn. They should be washed and then used raw in mixed salads or as a garnish for soups.

*Historical Uses:* Hairy bittercress was at one time believed to strengthen the heart, helping to prevent cardiac diseases. It has been little used in either cookery or medicine, although extract of the leaves has been listed as a cure for minor stomach ailments, such as indigestion, and the flowers are said to have been used to treat cases of epilepsy.

*Scientific Notes:* Hairy bittercress is part of the cabbage family (Brassicaceae). It has not been the subject of much scientific interest, although it has been observed that the plant will grow better in areas that are well frequented by earthworms.

Wall pennywort (p. 40).

Hairy bittercress (p. 41).

Ivy-leaved toadflax (opposite).

## Ivy-leaved Toadflax – *Cymbalaria muralis*

> 'It is said to be found wild upon thatch'd houses in the north, and in Lancashire plentifully.'
>
> James Petiver, 1714

- Alternative Names: Ivy Calf-snout, Kenilworth Ivy, Wall Pepper
- Etymology: Greek, *cymbal*, a cymbal
- Perennial; on walls and rocks across the British Isles (rarer in northern Scotland). It has distinctive yellow, white and lilac flowers and, as the name implies, small ivy-shaped leaves.

Ivy-leaved toadflax is an imported species from southern Europe that, in historical times, escaped from gardens to become a naturalised British plant. It is generally found on rocky ground or, more commonly, on walls where it produces long trailing stems. Although called toadflax, this plant is not directly related to the other British species of toadflax (*Linaria* spp.), which are entirely different in character and considered to be a weed by many gardeners.

The leaves are small and fleshy with a powerful, bitter taste that lingers in the mouth for some time after eating. I must confess that this flavour does not appeal much to me but I know other foragers who rate ivy-leaved toadflax as a salad ingredient. The leaves should be picked in spring and summer.

*Cookery:* The broad leaves should be picked during the spring and summer when they are fresh and succulent. The leaves may be quite bitter and are best used raw as a minor ingredient within salads, but they may also be chopped and added sparingly to cooked pasta and rice dishes as well as stir-fries.

*Historical Uses:* Ivy-leaved toadflax does not feature in any of the historical herbalist treatises and was noted, in one nineteenth-century botanical work, as having no known medicinal properties. It has been suggested that some historical herbalists might have confused this plant with the wall pennywort, but the two are very different.

*Scientific Notes:* Ivy-leaved toadflax is part of the figwort family (Scorphulariaceae) and is related to the speedwell group of plants. The plant has not been investigated for its pharmaceutical properties but it is known to have high levels of flavonoids, natural antioxidant compounds which are believed to be generally beneficial to health.

## Greater Plantain – *Plantago major*

> 'No great dependence is at present placed on its healing powers.'
>
> James Smith, 1803

- Etymology: Latin, *planta*, a plant
- Perennial; common in untended gardens and fields across the British Isles. It has green flowers and broad, egg-shaped leaves with long grooved stalks.

Viewed as something of a menace by most gardeners, the greater plantain is a sizeable weed that may be found on disturbed ground and neglected flowerbeds as well as fields and grassy verges. The leaves are edible and may be gathered in the spring and summer but the taste is really quite unpleasant. I suspect that most foragers will try eating it just the once.

*Cookery:* Historically the leaves of plantains would be picked, washed, boiled and served as greens but this must surely have been as a last resort. The plant is very bitter with a saline taste which, when combined with the toughness of its leaves (even after extended cooking), renders it barely edible. As if this is not enough, ingestion of large quantities of the plant may have a laxative effect.

As an alternative to eating it, some modern herbalists prepare a plantain tea using a spoonful of dried leaves or root which is placed into a cup with boiling water. Many health properties are claimed for this tea but it has the same bitter taste as the raw plant.

*Historical Uses:* In historical times plantain leaves were often applied to wounds and skin sores to stem bleeding. Expressed juice from the plant would be taken internally to help with ulcers, internal bleeding, dysentery and various pulmonary diseases, such as the coughing of blood. Modern herbalists often use the plant for treating various infectious diseases from colds to viral hepatitis.

*Scientific Notes:* The greater plantain is one of several related species within the family Plantaginaceae. The plant is known to contain a number of active biological compounds such as polysaccharides, lipids, flavonoids and caffeic acid derivatives. A pharmacological study of its compounds has suggested that the plant might hold the following medical properties: anti-inflammatory; wound healing; analgesic; antioxidant; antibiotic. The anti-viral properties of the greater plantain have been tested in the laboratory and, while the whole plant has no measurable effect, concentrations of some of its compounds did have some effect on bacteria and virus cultures. A 1992 trial indicated that chewing dried greater plantain leaves produced an aversion to tobacco, even in heavy smokers, and the plant has been suggested as being of potential help to those wishing to quit their cigarette habit.

## Biting Stonecrop – *Sedum acre*

'It is so harmless a herb that you can scarce use it amiss.'
Nicholas Culpeper, 1652

- Alternative Names: Goldmoss Stonecrop, Wall Pepper, Wall Ginger
- Etymology: Latin, *sedeo*, to sit, from the way the plant grows
- Perennial; on stones, walls, rocks and gravel across the British Isles. It has small yellow flowers and blunt, fleshy, egg-shaped leaves.

This pretty trailing plant is often cultivated in hanging baskets or on rockeries (as are other stonecrop species; in fact, there are entire societies devoted to growing these plants), but it may also be commonly found in the wild. I have found it to be common in coastal regions where it may grow in light, sandy soils and on the tops of sea walls.

Biting stonecrop has a strong peppery flavour that gives way to a sour aftertaste which may linger for a while. It is not a plant to be eaten on its own but it does make an exciting addition to certain dishes. The leaves should be picked in the spring or early summer.

*Cookery:* The leaves of biting stonecrop may be gathered at any time of the year although they are perhaps at their best in the spring, just before the distinctive yellow flowers appear. After washing, the leaves may be used raw to add a peppery taste to salads or a peppery garnish to soups and light dishes of pasta, and I have added it to home-made pizzas with success. The taste may not be to everyone's liking, and the plant is best used sparingly to add bite to a dish rather than as a central flavour.

*Historical Uses:* Historically biting stonecrop has been applied to injuries and ulcers including bleeding wounds, sores and haemorrhoids, internal haemorrhaging and other more serious conditions, including cancerous tumours. It was used to treat epilepsy in ancient times and was seen as a general tonic for coughs, colds and fevers. It is sometimes used as such by modern herbalists.

*Scientific Notes:* Biting stonecrop is part of the Crassulaceae family. It (and other species in the *Sedum* genus) contains a number of alkaloid compounds which have been periodically investigated by members of the biochemical community. However, the plant itself has not been clinically tested and is not generally thought to hold measurable medicinal properties. There are suggestions that the active compound which produces the peppery taste, piperidine, is toxic when ingested in large doses.

**Above:** *Plantain leaves (p. 44).*

**Right:** *Rosebay willowherb (opposite).*

*Biting stonecrop (p. 45).*

## Rosebay Willowherb – *Chamerion (Epilobium) angustifolium*

> 'There is an elegance in the rusticity of this plant and the liveliness of its flower that are seldom surpassed by the choicest gifts of Flora.'
>
> Henry Philips, 1829

- Alternative Names: French Willow, Fireweed, Loosestrife
- Perennial; common on recently-disturbed ground and waste areas across the British Isles. It has pink flowers and leaf veins which form into circular loops that join together.

This rather beautiful plant is quick to colonise vacant patches of soil and is known by some as fireweed because it is one of the first plants to grow on scorched ground following furze and forest fires. Many of the earlier botanical works list the plant as being rare but this is certainly not the case nowadays. The edible qualities of the plant are somewhat questionable but the leaves may be foraged for in the spring.

*Cookery:* Harvest the shoots and roots of rosebay willowherb in the springtime before the plant flowers (the mature plant is bitter, tough and inedible). In general the plant has a bitter taste that may not be to everyone's liking but this may be lessened by effective trimming/peeling/scraping and, in the case of the roots, by removing the brown thread inside.

The plant is best prepared by cutting the shoots and roots into short lengths and then boiling for several minutes until tender. Serve them like asparagus, with melted butter, salt and pepper. Rosebay willowherb should be used as a side dish to accompany roast meat or vegetables. (See Introduction regarding the uprooting of wild plants.)

*Historical Uses:* Some herbalists dismissed willowherb as being a plant of the 'bastard kind' while others, including John Gerard, esteemed it. It seems that its main function was not as an herbal medicine but as a killer of annoying flying insects, such as gnats, and as a repellent of snakes. This would be achieved by burning the dried plant. Gerard also affirms that it has the power to dye hair yellow.

*Scientific Notes:* Rosebay willowherb is part of the wider willowherb family (Onograceae). The scientific community's main interest in rosebay willowherb concerns certain complicated chemical peculiarities relating to its reproductive cycle, but it has not been investigated for any pharmaceutical or medical properties.

## Red and White Dead Nettles – *Lamium purpureum; L. album*

Both are of the white dead nettle]

'No less common a weed in cultivated ground as in untilled places.'
James Smith, 1803

- Alternative Names: Red Archangel, Dee Nettle, White Archangel
- Etymology: Greek, *laimos*, the throat, from the shape of the flowers
- Annual; gardens and waste ground across all of Britain. White or purple/pink flowers and heart-shaped leaves.

The red and white dead nettles have leaves that resemble the more familiar and feared stinging nettle but both are completely harmless, hence the name. They are a common coloniser of flower-beds and cultivated ground and are listed as weeds in many gardening manuals. They should not be confused with the henbit dead nettle (*L. amplexicaule*), alongside which it frequently grows and which, while edible, is inferior. (The red and white dead nettles have stalked leaves.) The dead nettles have a strong aromatic smell when crushed between the fingers.

*Cookery:* Dead nettles may produce flowers at any time of the year but it is in the spring that the leaves are fresh and at their best, at which time they should preferably be taken from the top of the plant. Historically dead nettle leaves have not been used in any specific recipes but would instead be washed, then lightly boiled and served with melted butter to form a vegetable side dish. They may also be used as a raw ingredient in salads or as an aromatic addition to vegetable soups.

*Historical Uses:* In historical times herbalists would use the young leaves and flowers of dead nettles to treat a variety of lesser illnesses such as stomach cramps and indigestion, as well as more serious conditions such as scrofula and ulcerated wounds.

*Scientific Notes:* The dead nettles are part of the family Lamiaceae which contains a number of similar-looking species. Laboratory experiments suggest that some species of *Lamium* have antifungal properties and that *L. album* might have compounds which could help prevent anaemia, although in neither case have these findings been afforded any useful medical properties.

## Stingless Nettle

## Stinging Nettle – *Urtica dioica; U. urens*

> 'A sick sheep must be forced to eat nettles; and when it has so done, the shepherd should piss into its mouth.'
>
> William Ellis, 1749

- Etymology: Latin, *uro*, to burn, from its stinging qualities
- Perennial; very common on disturbed and waste ground across the British Isles. It has green flowers and distinctive, serrated hairy leaves.

The stinging nettle will need little introduction as most of us learn to recognise and then avoid this prolific and painful plant at an early age. Nettles prefer to grow in disturbed, nitrogen-rich soil and so have a long association with human civilisation, so much so that archaeologists use nettles as an indicator of past activity when surveying new sites.

There are two species of British nettle, the common nettle (*Urtica dioica*) and the small nettle (*Urtica urens*), both of which are widespread and may be found in the rich soil of gardens and wastelands as well as hedgerows and woodlands. Given their painful nature, it may seem perverse that nettles should be edible at all, let alone be a good source of free food. Yet edible they are, and if cooked properly, nettles possess a bitter but aromatic taste that will suit many palates. Given their abundance in urban and rural environments, the nettle should be a classic target for the suitably gloved forager. Its young leaves, once cooked, may be used as an ingredient in a number of dishes.

*Cookery:* Although sometimes the butt of jokes about foraging, the stinging nettle was not widely used as a direct food source in historical times. In early recipe books nettles are mostly mentioned as part of medical cures, not mainstream cookery. The nettle was not a widely liked plant and, although it was grown for use in the paper and textile industries, many ordinary farmers did their utmost to get rid of the plant lest they be afforded the insulting title of 'cultivator of nettles'.

It is claimed that the Scots were the most prolific users of nettles, regularly picking and boiling up the young leaves to make nettle soup, nettle pudding and nettle porridge. At least one of these recipes travelled further south as the diarist Samuel Pepys records eating nettle porridge in 1661. However, by the nineteenth century the nettle is little referenced in culinary terms except as an additive to a select few recipes.

One such is the 'nettle cheese' of Cheshire, so called because a new cheese would be laid out upon a bed of fine, young nettle leaves which would be changed daily for a fortnight until it ripened. Doing so would afford the finished cheese 'an exceedingly fine and smooth coat' which according to one 1668 source, creates the 'finest summer cheese which can be eaten'. This recipe is by far the most widely quoted domestic use for nettles and is reproduced in several nineteenth-century cookery books, although later versions recommend ash leaves as a substitute.

*White dead nettle (p. 48).*

*Stinging nettle (p. 49).*

In more modern times the inclusion of nettles as an ingredient in domestic cookery increased markedly. Some of these recipes are based on traditional dishes, such as nettle porridge and nettle cheese; others are more modern in origin. In either case the nettle can be used to form delicious and nutritious dishes for everyday use.

Both British species of nettle are prepared and eaten in the same manner, the trick being to pick (using stout gloves and scissors) only the youngest, freshest shoots and leaves in the springtime, before the plant starts to flower. Most recipes require a good number of nettles, so for a family meal be prepared to gather a large bag full of leaves, all of which should be washed or soaked and any remaining stalks carefully removed.

In general terms, nettles will act as an excellent substitute for spinach in recipes, the cooked leaves (which cannot sting) taking on approximately the same texture. This means that roughly chopped nettles, when boiled, can be used as a spinach substitute in everyday dishes such as risotto and pasta. More specific recipes are rather far and few between but a firm favourite is nettle soup, a delicious version of which is presented below.

*NETTLE AND POTATO SOUP*

Add a good-sized knob of butter to a large pot and melt over a medium heat. Add one chopped onion and fry until opaque. Add 1500ml of vegetable stock and 500g of peeled, diced potatoes. Bring to the boil and simmer for 10–15 mins, until the potatoes are soft. Add approximately 600g of washed, chopped nettles and cook for another 10–15 mins.

*Lime tree leaves and blossom (p. 52).*

Add seasoning to taste and purée to a fine texture using a hand blender, food processor or similar. Add 100ml of cream if desired and serve.

*Historical Uses:* A survey of historical published recipes reveals that nettles were not commonly used as a source of nutrition, but instead as part of a 'physick' or curative herbal potion. This applies both to humans and animals as the earlier quote by William Ellis demonstrates.

Human curatives generally require the nettle leaves to be boiled up and then strained, the juice being combined with either sugar or honey as part of a treatment for lung diseases such as asthma, phlegm and tuberculosis. Herbalists also offer nettles as 'a remedy against the stinging of venomous creatures, the biting of mad dogs and the poisonous qualities of hemlock, henbane, nightshade and mandrake', as well as an antiseptic for open sores and wounds.

*SYRUP OF NETTLES (1749 recipe)*

Take the red nettles in the spring of the year; pick and wash them very clean through two or three waters; beat them in a mortar, and squeeze out the juice; let it stand twenty-four hours to fettle; then pour all the clear juice from the grounds. To every mutchkin (quarter pint) of juice take a pound of sugar-candy, and clarify it; boil and scum it, and, when cold, bottle it up.

*Scientific Notes:* Stinging nettles belong to the Urticaceae family. They have high levels of antioxidant compounds and potassium, so much so that fears have been expressed that excessive consumption could lead to heightened potassium levels in the blood. Stinging nettles have sometimes been recommended to help ease some of the sexual dysfunctional symptoms that accompany prostate problems, but clinical trials have found no evidence to support this idea. There is, however, some evidence that compounds found in nettles may help reduce inflammation in cases of arthritis and that they might have anti-ulcer, antimicrobial and (ironically) painkilling properties (the exact usefulness of nettles in these respects remains a matter of scientific debate).

## Lime Tree – *Tilia europaea; T. cordata*

- Etymology: Greek, *pteleia*, an elm
- Tree; *T. europaea* is commonly found in towns, villages and parks all around the British Isles, while *T. cordata* is found in the wild mainly in southern Britain.

The common lime tree (*T. europaea*) is a hybrid species that is commonly planted in parks, on village greens and along urban streets, while the small-leafed lime (*T. cordata*) is a wild counterpart. The lime tree's habit of dropping sticky honeydew deposits does not endear it to those who park their cars beneath them. Consequently the trees are frequently subjected to severe pollarding, especially in urban areas. The flowers are used to form linden tea and should be gathered in the late spring when they are young and fresh.

*Cookery:* The principal attraction of the lime tree to herbalists is as a source of linden tea, a pleasant drink with an aromatic floral taste that was at one time prescribed as a relaxant and a cure for fevers.

Linden tea is made from lime blossom which appears near the end of June and must be picked and dried before use. The tea is made by adding hot water to a few dried flowers (about a gram in weight) in a cup. Allow to infuse for several minutes then strain and, if desired, add sugar or honey. Alternatively, linden tea bags are available from some health food shops. Young lime leaves may be eaten raw and have been described in historical texts as a salad leaf, but personally I have not found them to be all that appealing.

*Historical Uses:* Extracts of lime leaves and flowers have been used to help in a variety of disorders including headaches, coughs, infections, fevers and hypertension. Lime tea was often used to calm the nerves or to treat convulsions or episodes of hysteria. Modern herbalists prefer to use the leaves and flowers of the small-leaved lime (*T. cordata*) as these are believed to be more potent than those of the hybridised common lime.

*Scientific Notes:* The lime tree resides in the lime family (Tiliaceae) with *T. europaea* being a hybrid of the species *T. platyphyllos* and *T. cordata*. Lime flowers are high in the antioxidant compounds flavonoids and there are indications that extracts from trees in the *Tilia* genus (especially *T. cordata*) may be beneficial to the liver. Other medical properties ascribed to lime trees have either not been proven or have yet to be tested.

# *Chapter Two*

# Hedgerows and Meadows

Britain's countryside is justly famous for its patchwork of fields and meadows, many of which are bordered by dense hedgerows and earthy banks. These beautiful features are surprisingly complex and play an important part in countryside ecology. Some may be home to hundreds of species of plant and animal.

One might think that there could be few places that are more wild and natural but it should be borne in mind that ultimately hedges, meadows and banks are all artificial features imposed on the landscape by the necessities of agriculture. Even so, some of our hedgerows were founded hundreds or even thousands of years ago and in Britain's overcrowded countryside, they have become ecosystems in their own right. They also have an important role in the movement of wildlife, acting as green corridors across the landscape along which species of plant and animal may travel.

The open nature of most hedgerows and meadows allows sunlight and rain to fall upon the ground, encouraging a rapid and diverse growth of plants. Large shrubs and tall-growing or sprawling plants (such as hawthorn and cleavers) will be obvious and may be spotted while strolling through the countryside. However, when left to its own devices, vegetation along a path or roadside can become dense and overgrown, especially during the springtime and summer. This can make it difficult to differentiate individual plants from among the tangle and it is often necessary to stop and make a deliberate search for smaller or less common plants which may be growing among grass or beneath other broad-leaved plants. I generally set aside a couple of hours for a hedgerow-foraging session and will plan my route in advance, choosing public rights-of-way, green lanes or little-used roads which are lined with hedges, earth banks or pass through meadows or fallow pasture. It goes without saying that our fields and hedges need to be treated with great respect. Post-war agricultural subsidies encouraged the wholesale destruction of hedgerows, an error that has only recently been realised. This means that some hedgerows are in a neglected state; don't compound the problem by acting irresponsibly.

The usual precautions apply. Don't trespass (take an OS Map with you), take only what you need and be wary of potential sources of pollutants. In this respect, it is better to avoid gathering from the edges of cultivated fields as there is a risk of pesticides and herbicides having been sprayed. It is also wise not to forage in fields with dense livestock as their dung and urine may contain unwelcome bacteria. If possible, gather plants from areas that are unlikely to have suffered widespread disturbance and which are above the level

*The British countryside at its most colourful and edible.*

*Agrimony (opposite).*

of a dog's cocked leg. Wash all plants thoroughly. If by any chance you are approached by a farmer or landowner who objects to you foraging close to their property, apologise profusely and explain what you are doing: most (but not all) people will be sympathetic towards a humble forager.

## Agrimony – *Agrimonia eupatoria*

> 'The common agrimony is a very useful plant whose virtues are much neglected.'
>
> Nicholas Culpeper, 1652

- Etymology: Greek, *agremone*, a plant said to cure cataracts
- Perennial; common in grassy verges and hedgerows across the British Isles (but rare in far north). Yellow flowers, serrated leaves, burr-like fruits.

This rather attractive plant is noted for its yellow summer flowers and burr-like autumn fruits. Agrimony has a fruity but slightly bitter taste which does not make for good eating but does produce a pleasant herbal infusion.

*Cookery:* Although agreeable-smelling, agrimony is not really suitable for eating but its leaves and flowers may be gathered during the late spring and summer and dried for later use in herbal infusions.

Agrimony tea can be made by placing several leaves or flowers in about 250ml of boiling water. Allow the flavour to infuse, then strain away the leaves and add either sugar or honey to balance the taste. Older recipe books recommend boiling the leaves in a cooking pot, then allowing the mixture to grow cold before straining and drinking it.

*Historical Uses:* In historical times agrimony was widely used to treat liver and spleen disorders, to purify the blood and for instances of internal bleeding. By the nineteenth century the plant was not being recommended for serious complaints but it would still be given, in the form of tea, as a cure for insomnia or, as a gargle, for sore throats. The scientific name suggests that at one time the plant was used to treat eye cataracts.

*Scientific Notes:* Agrimony is part of the rose family (Rosaceae). The plant has high levels of antioxidants (especially flavonoids) and there is limited evidence that extracts from the plant possess an antibacterial quality. Clinical trials suggest that the dried leaves do not assist in the treatment of diabetes, as is sometimes claimed.

## Blackthorn – *Prunus spinosa*

> 'It is alleged that the "rough-flavoured teas" of cheap dealers are more indebted for their roughness to the sloe, than to any ingredient from China.'
>
> *British Encyclopedia*, 1829

- Alternative Names: Sloe, Scrog, Slon Tree
- Etymology: Greek, *proune*, a plum
- Large shrub; found in hedgerows across Britain (except very far north). White flowers, purple-black berries, branches thorny.

A common and widespread tall shrub that may be seen in hedgerows and coppices. Blackthorn was once widely grown as cover for game birds and so is often associated with parts of the countryside that are, or were, managed for shooting parties. The most famous product of the blackthorn is its purple-black fruit, known as sloes, which festoon the branches in the autumn and which are traditionally picked following the first winter frost. Gathering sloes used to be a common seasonal pastime but in recent decades the practice has gone out of fashion and it is not uncommon to see some trees burdened with a great weight of unwanted fruit.

*Cookery:* Sloe berries do not taste great on their own and so must be cooked with other ingredients. Historically there are two main uses for sloe: as the principal ingredient in a rather acerbic conserve, and as a flavouring for the alcoholic drink 'sloe gin'.

Sloe conserve is not a great delicacy and relies on the addition of much sugar to mask the rather acerbic taste of the fruit. In fairness, sloe conserve was never meant to be an everyday food but was mostly used as a medicinal aid to digestion.

*SLOE CONSERVE (1814 recipe)*

Put the sloes in water upon the fire, that they may soften, taking care that they be not broken. Then take them out of the water, press out the pulp, and mix it with three times its weight of double refined sugar. Boil into a conserve and bottle. (See introductory section for advice on jam-making.)

*SLOE GIN*

Sloe gin is well known and tastes great. Ironically, the practice of adding sloes to gin probably arose in a bid to mask the taste of cheap or doctored spirits, but the recipe works very well indeed with modern branded gin and vodka.

Sloe gin requires gathering ripe fruit (the riper the better) which must then be thoroughly washed. Tradition says that each berry should be individually pricked using a thorn from the blackthorn tree but placing them in a freezer overnight and then defrosting will have the same effect.

Take a wide-mouthed preserving jar (e.g. a Kilner jar) and half fill it with the pricked/defrosted sloes. Measure out your gin (or vodka, either will be fine) and for each litre add 200g of sugar. Pour the spirits over the sloes and add a sprinkling of spices such as cloves and cinnamon. Seal the jar and shake it to mix the sloes, sugar and spirits; thereafter invert the jar once a day for at least two weeks, then once a week for a further three to four months. After this the liquid can be carefully decanted or siphoned into bottles, leaving any fruit and sediment behind. The remaining gin-soaked sloes may be boiled with sugar and turned into jam.

In 1938 the writer George Orwell was given a more traditional sloe gin recipe by some Hampshire travellers: 'Pick your sloes when they be fine and ripe, with dry air, and warm with the sun. Prick each one with a needle three times. Take half a bottle of unsweetened gin and put in a fistful of sugar-candy, firm and strong, the taste of a crushed bitter almond, or the kernels of ripe apricots, crushed. Fill the bottle with the sloes and press them down. If you be not on the road, lay beneath the floor of your tent where you be sleeping, for they slags (sloes) dunnot like the cold. Let 'em bide till Christmas come, when take out the fruit and let 'em bide till you need 'em.'

*Historical Uses:* Although the sloes are the most obvious part of the tree for foragers, in times past the flowers and bark would be gathered and dried by herbalists for use in purgative medicines such as laxatives. The unripe sloes were said to have a similar herbalist quality and would be boiled into a thick syrup that was known to apothecaries as 'German acacia'. Sloe juice has also been used as an ink and it is said that dried blackthorn leaves were at one time used by grocers to adulterate their stock of tea.

*Scientific Notes:* Blackthorn is part of the rose family (Rosaceae). It has not been clinically assessed for its medical properties but in rare instances it has been known to irritate the skin of those who get scratched by the thorns.

## Cleavers – *Galium aparine*

> 'She slyly adorned her friends with cleavers, and laughed to see their repeatedly vain endeavours to escape from their tenacious hold.'
>
> James Northcote, 1829

- Alternative Names: Goosegrass, Robin-run-the-hedge, Gooseshare, Aparine, Stickyweed, Stickywilly, Catchweed, Coachweed
- Etymology: Greek, *gala*, milk, which the plant was used to curdle
- Annual; abundant in hedgerows, gardens and uncultivated land across Britain. White flowers; long straggly tendrils with sticky stems and leaves.

Once described as a 'pretty toy of childhood', cleavers is instantly recognisable for its lengthy tendrils which are covered in prickly Velcro-like hooks which allow it to cling

Sloes, fruit of the blackthorn (p. 56).

Cleavers (p. 57 and opposite).

to clothing. For centuries this stickiness has been exploited by schoolchildren who gain delight from deftly placing a length of cleavers onto the back of an unwitting victim, then watch with delight as they try to remove it.

Many gardeners will be familiar with cleavers as a rapidly growing summer weed that will quickly choke a flower-bed or vegetable plot if left untended for a small length of time. Even in historical times this plant was not well-liked and caused the herbalist Nicholas Culpeper to remark that: 'It is so troublesome an inhabitant in gardens, that it rampeth upon, and is ready to choak whatever grows near it.' Cleavers has a green vegetable taste, and will often form a dense, tangled carpet of vegetation in ditches, hedgerows and neglected parts of gardens.

*Cookery:* Cleavers is eaten by many animals (especially geese) but it is not generally popular as a source of domestic food, probably because of its hairiness (which lessens with cooking) and tough, fibrous texture. The plant should be foraged in early spring before the burrs appear. It is inedible when raw, so strip the leaves from the stalk and wash, then roughly chop them before boiling or steaming for several minutes until tender. They may then be strained and used as a green side vegetable.

The plant's fruit (small spiky burrs), when dried, roasted in a medium oven until brown and then ground, may be used as a substitute for coffee but the effort needed to do this is scarcely worth it. A better drink is cleaver's tea which was at one time recommended as a health tonic, especially for those dieting.

*CLEAVERS TEA (1837 recipe)*
Take of the leaves and stalks of cleavers, two ounces (56g). Add two pints (1.1 litres) of water then boil gently until reduced to a pint (570ml). A tea-cupful to half a pint (280ml) is to be taken three times a day.

*Historical Uses:* Apothecaries endowed cleavers with many remarkable properties including the ability to cure certain cancers and as an antidote to the poisonous bite of an adder. However, its principal use by apothecaries was to help ease the symptoms of jaundice, dysentery, earache and ulcerated wounds. Even in more modern times it has been cited as being a 'blood purifier' and, in 1883, was cited as a cure for chronic ulcers by a well-known British medic.

*Scientific Notes:* Cleavers is part of the bedstraw family (Rubiaceae) and as such is related to the coffee plant. Few of the many medicinal claims made for cleavers have been substantiated but a recent study does suggest that the plant has considerable antibacterial and antifungal qualities.

## Common Sorrel – *Rumex acetosa*

> 'The whole herb is acid, with a degree of astringency, not unpleasant nor unwholesome.'
> Philip Miller, 1835

- Alternative Names: Garden Sorrel, Spinach Dock, Narrow-leaved Dock
- Etymology: Latin, *rumex*, the old name for sorrel
- Perennial; hedgerows and grassy areas across Britain. Flowers reddish on tall spikes; leaves ovate and pointed.

Common sorrel is a wild plant which may be very common in hedgerows and on cultivated land and in times past it was grown in gardens as an herb. The young leaves have a pleasant acidic taste comparable to sour fruits or vinegar and should be gathered during the spring.

*Cookery:* Historically sorrel leaves have been eaten raw in salads (often as a means of avoiding scurvy) or boiled up in milk to form a flavoured whey. The juice from the plant was also diluted and then refrigerated, to form a cool summer drink.

In modern cookery common sorrel has been overlooked for the calmer flavour of the domestic French sorrel (*Rumex scutatus*). Common sorrel is, however, a versatile herb that can be used raw in salads, although its sharp acidic taste may not suit those not used to the delights of eating wild plants. In my experience sorrel is better when used sparingly as an herb to flavour soups and pasta dishes. To do this simply gather a handful of leaves, wash, chop and boil them, then purée the mixture into a pesto.

*Historical Uses:* Herbalists believed that sorrel was an excellent blood purifier and could be used to treat heatstroke, heat rash, dehydration, parasitic worms and period pains. All parts of the plant would be used and either turned into a drink or desiccated into powdered form. It is also alleged that sorrel root can alleviate the effects of a scorpion's sting and, when dried, used to take out creases when ironing. Sorrel is currently recommended for use as a mild laxative and in cases of kidney stones (but see below).

*Scientific Notes:* Sorrel is part of the knotweed family (Polygonaceae). The leaves are high in fibre and laboratory tests on rats suggest that the plant may have a 'high nutritive value', it having promoted growth in animals which were fed on it. A detailed analysis of nineteen organic compounds found in sorrel suggests that it has high levels of oxalic acid, a substance that can be associated with kidney stones and other digestive troubles.

## Garlic Mustard – *Alliaria petiolata*

> 'The fresh leaves eaten as salad work by urine powerfully, and are recommended in dropsies.'
>
> John Hill, 1812

- Alternative Names: Jack-by-the-hedge, Garlic Root, Sauce Alone, Hedge Garlic, Sauce-alone, Jack-in-the-bush, Penny Hedge, Poor Man's Mustard
- Etymology: Latin, *all*, pungent, because of its scent
- Biennial; hedgerows and waste ground across Britain (except north Scotland). White flowers, distinctive heart-shaped leaves which smell of garlic.

Historically known as Jack-by-the-hedge, the garlic mustard plant takes its name from the mild garlic and mustard flavour possessed by its leaves, flowers and fruit. It was once widely used to flavour sauces and was especially popular as an accompaniment to sea fish, it being believed that the plant helped to counteract any 'corrupt humours' lurking in the dish. The young leaves smell faintly of garlic when crushed and are best gathered during the spring. Be warned that the plant has a reputation for giving foul-smelling breath to those who eat it raw.

*Cookery:* The plant was at one time widely eaten with one eighteenth-century botanist noting that 'when gathered as it approaches the flowering state, boiled separately, and then eaten to boiled mutton, it certainly forms a most desirable potherb and to any kind of salted meat, an excellent green.'

Garlic mustard leaves may be gathered at any time but they are at their best in the spring, before the plant flowers. When washed and chopped the leaves may be eaten raw in salads, in sandwiches or on bread and butter. They may also be boiled to form a side vegetable and, in times past, would be used in cooked sauces to accompany fish and meat dishes.

One common use for garlic mustard is in a pesto which may be used raw on toast or added to pasta and especially fish dishes. To make this take two large bunches of washed and shaken garlic mustard leaves; place these in a food processor with two garlic cloves and a handful of walnuts. Blend into a smooth paste then add 10–12 tablespoons of olive oil; blend again then add a generous amount of grated Parmesan cheese, salt and pepper and blend again.

*Historical Uses:* As an herbal remedy it was the plant's seeds that were considered to be of the greatest value. These would usually be picked, bruised and then boiled in wine or honey to produce a drink which was said to be of use with colic, coughs, digestive trouble and circulation disorders. The leaves would also be applied to cuts and wounds as an antiseptic.

Common sorrel (p. 60).

Ground ivy (opposite).

Garlic mustard (p. 61).

*Scientific Notes:* Garlic mustard is part of the cabbage family (Brassicaceae). It is a rapidly spreading invasive species which is thought to dislodge competing plants by disrupting their ability to germinate and/or interfering with the root growth. It is also thought to have the ability to kill insect larvae. Laboratory tests reveal garlic mustard to have powerful antioxidants; these compounds are noted for their ability to remove damaging free radicals from the body, although the exact medical benefits of this are still a matter of debate.

## Ground Ivy – *Glechoma hederacea*

> 'Ground ivy is hot and dry in the first degree from its quick, sharp and bitter taste.'
>
> Edward Baylis, 1791

- Alternative Names: Creeping Charlie, Catsfoot, Field Balm, Run-away-robin, Gill-over-the-ground, Alehoof, Tunhoof
- Perennial; common in hedgerows and grasslands across the British Isles. Flowers violet and tubular, rounded leaves on stalks.

Ground ivy was once widely used in the brewing industry and was consequently known as alehoof and tunhoof in some parts of Britain. When bruised it emits an aromatic smell but the plant tastes far too bitter to be eaten raw or in general cookery, although it can be used to make a pleasant herbal infusion. Its leaves and stems should be gathered during the spring and summer.

*Cookery:* Too bitter to be eaten, ground ivy may be turned into an agreeable herbal infusion. Pick the leaves and stems in the spring or early summer. Wash and then bruise them before placing in a teapot or cup of boiling water for several minutes. After straining you can add either sugar or honey, according to taste. The leaves may be dried and stored in an airtight container. Some historical recipes for 'gill tea' recommend combining ground ivy with chamomile.

*Historical Uses:* Apothecaries were attracted by strong-smelling plants such as ground ivy and the plant has a long list of aliments for which it could be prescribed. These range from headaches, coughs, colds and colic through to bladder and kidney disorders. It is even recommended for hypochondriacs! Ground ivy was usually taken in the form of a tea or syrup but it would also be dried and used as snuff.

*Scientific Notes:* Ground ivy is part of the dead nettle family (Lamiaceae). Its leaves contain a unique lectin compound called gleheda which acts as a powerful insecticide. Other preliminary laboratory-based investigations have raised the possibility that compounds within ground ivy might be useful in certain instances of disease-related inflammation. The plant chemistry as a whole is of interest because of the light that it has shed on the evolutionary history of certain vegetable-derived compounds.

## Hawthorn – *Crataegus monogyna*

'Dear hawthorn tree, thou bring'st to me
Tidings of hours 'tis bliss to see!
Thy milk-white glow, itself a show,
All rich with Evening's ruddy glow.'

Unknown poet, 1835

- Etymology: Greek, *cratos*, strength, from the hardness of the wood
- Small tree; forms hedges and thickets across Britain. White blossom, small leaves, thorny, clusters of bright red berries.

The hawthorn tree will probably need little introduction, it being a distinctive hedging plant that may commonly be seen bordering country lanes, fields and public rights-of-way. The bright, white petals of its flowers start to emerge in the spring and are sometimes referred to as 'May blossom', this being the month when it commonly occurs.

There is much folklore associated with the hawthorn, with perhaps the most famous tale being that of the Glastonbury thorn, a plant which was said to have been planted by Joseph of Arimathea and which flowered close to Christmas Day prior to its death in 1991. Another alleged Christmas Day hawthorn in the New Forest was disproved in 1786 when an investigating committee announced that 'no leaf is ever to be seen on it'. It is the red fruit, called haws, which are gathered from the plant during the late summer and early autumn.

*Cookery:* The distinctive red haws may be picked and used in various conserves and pickles. The berries should be ripe when picked and will need to be separated from their stalks before cooking. A quick way of doing this is to rub a bunch of haws between your hands; the stalks will break off leaving you with just the berries. There are also historical references to the flowers and young leaves being added to enhance the flavour of soups or sauces.

*HAW SAUCE*

Take around 500g of ripe haws which have been stripped from their bunches and well washed. Place in a pan with around 300ml of malt vinegar and simmer until the haws have broken down into a pulp (around 30–40 mins). Press through a sieve to remove any large fragments then add 70g of sugar and a generous quantity of salt and pepper. Return to the pan and boil for several minutes before bottling. Use as a condiment with roast dishes.

*HAW JELLY*

Take a kilo of ripe, washed, stripped haws and place in a large, heavy pan with about 600ml of water. Bring to the boil and cover, then simmer for at least an hour until the berries form a pulp. If necessary, help the process by mashing with a spoon or other utensil. Strain the mixture into a bowl using a muslin bag or similar; this may take several hours. Measure out the resultant liquid and place in a heavy pan; for each 500ml of liquid add 500g of sugar and a tablespoon of lemon juice. Bring the mixture to the boil, stirring to dissolve the sugar; keep boiling until the setting point is reached (see Preparation Technique for details of this). Place in cleaned jam jars and immediately seal. Leave for a week or so before eating.

*HAW LIQUEUR (1832 recipe)*
The full blossoms of the white thorn are to be picked dry and clean from the leaves and stalks, and as much put into a large bottle as it will hold lightly without pressing it down; it is then to be filled up with French brandy, and allowed to stand two or three months, when it must be decanted off, and sweetened with sugar. Without the sweetening, it is an excellent seasoning for puddings and custards.

*HAW TEA*
The haws may also be used to form an herbal drink by simply placing a small handful of ripe haws into a cup and adding boiling water. After about 10 mins the haws will have infused into the water and can be strained off and the resultant tea drunk with the addition of sugar or honey.

*Historical Uses:* The hawthorn's familiarity and association with the arrival of spring led to it becoming a regular ingredient in many traditional herbal formulations. On their own the haws and flowers would often be boiled to form a juice, while their seeds would be bruised, dried, powdered and dissolved in wine. In this form the hawthorn was used as an antiseptic, digestive aid and an antidote to bladder and kidney stones. The juice was also said to draw out splinters and other objects embedded in the skin, which is perhaps a reflection of the hazard of the plant's thorns when gathering the haws. In modern times the hawthorn has been cited as being of benefit to the heart and general wellbeing.

*Scientific Notes:* Like many hedging plants, hawthorn is a member of the rose family (Rosaceae). The plant contains a number of active polyphenolic compounds, including several types of flavonoid. An extract taken from hawthorn leaves and flowers has been marketed in Europe as being beneficial to those suffering from heart disease such as arrhythmia. This is probably linked to the clinical discovery that hawthorn extract has a measurable effect on the cardiovascular system and is known to widen the blood vessels.

*Horseradish root.*

*Haws, fruit of the hawthorn (p. 64).*

## Horseradish – *Armoracia rusticana*

> 'It stimulates the stomach, and assists digestion; beyond which their effects are also carried, as they promote both perspiration and urine.'
>
> William Nisbet, 1801

- Alternative Names: Mountain Radish, Great Raifort, Red Cole
- Etymology: Latin, *armoracia*, old name for this plant
- Perennial; generally cultivated but semi-wild populations may be found in damp hedgerows and ditches in southern Britain. White flowers, broad arrow-shaped leaves emerging from the root.

The horseradish plant is familiar to most people via the piquant, pungent sauce which has been used as an accompaniment to roast beef since at least the seventeenth century. Horseradish is not a native British plant but was probably introduced into the islands from south-eastern Europe. Its strong flavour has long endeared it to the human palate and the plant has been used as a food source since ancient times and was even cultivated for sale in local markets. It was particularly used in a finely grated form to flavour boiled cod and other white fish.

The horseradish plant may be found as semi-wild populations in hedgerows, fields and waste ground but it is also grown as a garden herb plant. Although the leaves are edible as boiled greens, they are not much of a delicacy and it is the plant's root that is generally sought, usually during the autumn and winter months. It has a hot, fiery taste which hits the back of the throat and may make the eyes water. It is not for the faint-hearted.

*Cookery:* Traditionally the best horseradish roots are obtained in November and they may be obtained by digging up the entire plant (but see Introduction regarding the legality of uprooting wild plants). Please note that horseradish sap is a notable skin irritant and is an especial nuisance to those who suffer from dermatitis.

After washing, the root may be stored for some months in a dry place, or the flesh may be preserved by finely grating it (be warned, this process may bring tears to the eyes) and then mixing it with white wine vinegar and a pinch of cayenne pepper. In this state it will keep in the fridge for some months. In the days before fridges the root would often be sliced, dried in a hot oven and then powdered. Grated horseradish that is not quickly mixed with vinegar will darken and become bitter.

In modern domestic situations horseradish may be used sparingly to add flavour to vegetable soups or some lighter Asian dishes such as green and coconut curries. It is, however, as a condiment that horseradish is best known and in this form it may be used to accompany beef, fish, boiled potatoes and other cooked dishes, according to the diner's taste. It may also be used in Japanese cookery as a substitute for wasabi sauce (which is based on a Japanese species of horseradish).

*TRADITIONAL HORSERADISH SAUCE*

Take a washed and prepared horseradish root and from it grate about 4 tablespoons of flesh. In a bowl mix it with a teaspoon each of sugar and salt, then add two teaspoons of mustard and a generous pinch of pepper. Moisten the mixture with vinegar until a creamy consistency is reached. The sauce may be used like this as a condiment or as an ingredient in soups, etc. For a more elegant presentation with roast dinners, stir in a small quantity of gently warmed cream.

*Historical Uses:* With such a strong taste, horseradish had to be used sparingly by herbalists who would often make it palatable by dissolving a small amount of the powdered root in wine or sugared water. Alternatively, strips of horseradish would be laid on an afflicted part of the body. Its common uses were as a cure for scurvy and joint problems or, when laid on the skin, to reduce swellings or hardness in the spleen and liver.

*Scientific Notes:* Horseradish is part of the cabbage family (Brassicaceae) of plants. For over a century various species of horseradish have been scientifically studied because they possess a compound called peroxidise. This is an enzyme that has a wide variety of industrial and commercial uses, such as in pollution control and as a substitute for corrosive chemicals in manufacturing. Analysis reveals the plant to be rich in vitamin C, potassium, calcium, magnesium and phosphorus, as well as the antibacterial agent named mustard oil.

## Primrose – *Primula vulgaris*

> 'And while he plucked the Primrose in its pride,
> He pondered o'er its bloom 'tween joy and pain;
> And a rude sonnet in its praise he tried,
> Where nature's simple way the aid of art supplied.'
>
> John Clare, 1821

- Etymology: Latin, *primus*, first, from its appearance in spring
- Perennial; in hedgerows, coppices and wild meadows across Britain. Solitary pale yellow flowers with darker centre; wrinkled leaves.

The appearance of the primrose has traditionally been greeted with joy in country areas as it is among the earliest of the spring flowers and, as such, signifies the close of winter (its name, primrose, means 'first rose'). The plant is distinctive and varieties of it have been domesticated for garden use.

In times gone by the flowers were picked to decorate houses and churches or for use in bouquets by florists. Although the whole plant is technically edible, the root is acrid and unpalatable and it is the leaves and flowers that should be foraged for during the spring, and used to add a floral flavour to salads and drinks.

*Cookery:* Historically, primrose flowers were used in drinks and would often be fermented with honey or sugar to create a fizzy alcoholic pick-me-up which was taken as 'a grateful summer beverage'. The primrose root would sometimes be added whole to casks of beer or wine to bolster the flavour (but see introductory section regarding the uprooting of wild plants).

Modern edible uses for the primrose are little different to those found in historical domestic cookbooks. The young leaves should be picked, washed and eaten raw in salads or boiled/steamed for use as a side vegetable. The young flowers can be steeped in hot water to make a pleasant tea, or added to a demijohn to enhance the flavour of white wine.

*PRIMROSE WINE (1822 recipe)*
Boil four pounds of moist sugar in ten quarts (11 litres) of water for about a quarter of an hour, and take off the scum. Then pour this on six pints (3.4 litres) of primroses, add some fresh yeast before it is quite cold, and let it work all night in a warm place. When the fermentation is over, close up the barrel, and still keep it in a warm place.

*Historical Uses:* Herbalists had few uses for primrose, although the flowers would be pressed onto the forehead to stop headaches and in the mouth for toothache. Its greatest reputation is as a narcotic with the juice of the flowers being said to help with insomnia and to relieve rheumatic and other bodily pains. Extract of the root was sometimes taken nasally as a form of snuff.

*Scientific Notes:* The common primrose is part of the wider family of primroses (Primulaceae) which includes cowslips and pimpernels. There has been little research into the medical or nutritional properties of the primrose and the plant seems to have been mostly of interest to members of the horticultural community.

## Tansy – *Tanacetum vulgare*

> 'I believe Asia does not afford a plant of greater flagrancy than tansy.'
>
> Herman Boerhaave, 1715

- Alternative Names: Bitter Buttons, Golden Buttons, Cow Bitter, Mugwort
- Etymology: Greek, *athanaton*, everlasting
- Perennial; hedgerows and waste ground across southern Britain. Yellow flowers, highly serrated leaves.

Tansy is fragrant and colourful but, while being edible, the plant must be treated with caution for within its leaves and flowers lurk a number of volatile oils which are highly toxic to insects and other invertebrates. While harmless at low doses, if tansy is eaten in sufficient quantity it may become injurious to humans, causing such problems as liver trouble and dermatitis. Consequently it should be consumed only in small quantities as a background flavouring in foods such as puddings and biscuits. The plant holds a bitter but aromatic taste and should be foraged for in the springtime.

*Cookery:* Tansy holds such a strong, pungent taste that it is of no surprise that this plant should have fallen out of favour with cooks. Indeed, it seems probable that in times past it was eaten only for its medical properties or because it was part of a tradition (e.g. tansy cakes eaten at Lent or after funerals).

In the sixteenth and seventeenth centuries tansy was used as an ingredient for cakes, omelettes and biscuits, with a favourite recipe being 'tansy pudding' (see below) which was traditionally eaten at Easter. It was also used to flavour spirits and to make a bitter tea (but see the fatal case quoted below). The herbalist Gerard recounts its use at Lent when tansy leaves would be added to eggs and flour to make cakes. However, by the turn of the nineteenth century tansy had fallen out of use, with several domestic books mentioning that it was a rarely used ingredient.

For those willing to give it a go, it is the young tansy leaves that should be picked during the late spring. They may then be washed, shredded and added (sparingly) to give flavour to sweet and savoury dishes such as cakes, puddings, pancakes and omelettes. Tansy was also used as a substitute for some spices, most notably cinnamon and nutmeg. The following historical recipe concerns tansy pudding: there were several versions of this recipe printed in the 1820s, suggesting that this dish was still being eaten regularly at this time.

Primrose (p. 68).

Tansy (p. 69).

Wild hops (opposite).

*TANSY PUDDING (1826 recipe)*
Beat seven eggs, yolks and whites separately. Add a pint (570ml) of cream, near the same of spinach-juice, and a little tansy-juice gained by pounding leaves in a stone mortar, a quarter of a pound (115g) of Naples biscuit, sugar to taste, a glass of white wine, and some nutmeg. Set all in a saucepan, just to thicken, over the fire; then put it into a dish lined with paste, to turn out, and bake it.

*Historical Uses:* The power of tansy may be demonstrated by its historical use as an insect repellent, most notably on dead bodies awaiting burial when sections of the plant would be placed in the nostrils and mouth to ward away flies. Indeed, in some parts of the country tansy was known as a funeral plant and was even called 'the immortal plant' on the European continent. Herbalists were aware of tansy's properties and ascribed many medical attributes to the plant but especially for digestive troubles, it being an effective cure for internal parasites such as tapeworms. It was also believed to be a cure for the mythical 'tooth worm' which was held responsible for a variety of diseases of the teeth and mouth. Other ascribed uses include as a cure for gout, migraines, flatulence and as a means of inducing a miscarriage. There are examples of fatal poisoning using tansy, including a case reported in an 1834 edition of *The Medical Magazine* which detailed the death of a 27-year-old woman who had ingested a large quantity of tansy tea.

*Scientific Notes:* Tansy is part of the daisy family (Asteraceae) and is closely related to the familiar marigold. It is suggested that tansy may contain chemicals which can cause allergic reactions leading to dermatitis. Oil distilled from tansy leaves has proved to be highly effective at repelling certain types of insect, most notably the Colorado beetle, a serious pest of potato plants, and certain types of tick.

## Wild Hops – *Humulus lupulus*

> 'The sun in the south, or else southerly and west,
> Is joy to the hop, as welcomed guest.
> But wind in the north, or else northerly east,
> To hop is as ill, as a fray in a feast.'
>
> Thomas Tusser, 1557

- Etymology: Latin, *humus*, fungal mould
- Perennial; semi-wild in hedgerows across lowland Britain. Climbing plant, leaves rough and opposing.

The sixteenth-century poet Thomas Tusser praised the hop plant and wrote (at length) about the skills required to grow and process it. In his day hops were just beginning to be grown commercially in Britain, although the plant itself had been cultivated on the continent since the Dark Ages and even used as a decorative garden plant by the Romans.

The main use of hops, then as now, was in the brewing industry, the plant's cones being carefully dried and then used in the fermentation of beer and ale.

*Cookery:* The young spring buds of wild plants would be picked, 'dressed as asparagus', then put in salads, while the summer flowers would sometimes be added to bread to assist the action of the yeast. One Victorian gardener writes: 'The young shoots, when they have risen three or four inches from the root, were formerly gathered and boiled like asparagus, to which they are very little inferior.'

The spring buds and shoots are the most palatable part of the wild hop plant and may be picked and then cooked by boiling. It may be served as a simple side dish or used as an ingredient in soups, pasta dishes and omelettes. One 1828 recipe directs that the young buds should 'be boiled in water, with a little salt, and eaten as a salad, with salt, pepper, oil, and vinegar'.

*Historical Uses:* The late Tudor herbalist Gerard wrote of beer that: 'The manifold virtues in hops do manifestly argue the wholesomeness of beer above ale; for the hops rather make it [a] physical drink to keep the body in health, than an ordinary drink for the quenching of our thirst.' As well as aiding the fermentation process, hops also acted as a preservative for the beer and, in this respect, replaced the use of ground ivy and wormwood in the brewing industry.

Modern physicians would probably disagree with the idea of beer being a health drink and by the eighteenth century it was recognised that there were two types of hops growing in Britain: the cultivated variety, grown commercially for the breweries; and the 'wild hedge hop' which would grow freely in the countryside. The first was perceived to have little medicinal or culinary value ('they are more toothsome than nourishing', wrote Gerard) while the second was believed to be useful for the internal organs, for purifying the blood and as a diuretic; it was still being recommended as a cure for gout in Victorian times. Hops extracts are still recommended as a cure for insomnia.

*Scientific Notes:* Wild hops are part of the hemp family (Cannabaceae) which means that they are related to the cannabis group of plants. Wild hops contain a number of active biological compounds, some of which have been investigated for potential medical effects. One of these, the flavonoid xanthohumol, has been investigated for possible anti-viral effects in relation to the HIV virus but the results, while not disheartening, require further clarification. A similar situation exists with other flavonoids from the female parts of the plant which have been tested in relation to ovarian and breast cancers and which have led to (very tentative) claims that taking hops-derived dietary supplements may help with the prevention of cancers. Related to this are studies on the oestrogenic effects of certain hops compounds, some of which are being investigated for possible pharmaceutical uses.

## Woodland (Wild) Strawberry – *Fragaria vesca*

'The strawberry grows underneath the nettle,
And wholesome berries thrive and ripen best
Neighboured by fruit of baser quality.'

Shakespeare, *Henry V*

- Etymology: Latin, *fragans*, fragrant, because of its scent
- Perennial; on grassy banks and dry fields across Britain. Pinkish flowers, low trailing plant.

The sweet succulence of the strawberry has attracted the human palate for thousands of years and there is evidence of their having been consumed during the Neolithic Era. By the time that Shakespeare was writing in praise of the strawberry, the plant had become a domesticated one whose fruit was fuller and juicier than its wild, uncultivated cousin. Indeed, there was some disagreement among the early botanists as to how many varieties of strawberry could be found in Britain, the estimates varying between three and seven. Nowadays there are two generally accepted plants, the familiar, but hybrid, garden strawberry, *Fragaria x ananassa* and the wild or woodland strawberry, *Fragaria vesca*. The two are very similar in taste and general appearance with the most obvious difference being in their fruits which, on the wild strawberry, are small and compact compared to those of the cultivated plant.

*Cookery:* There are, of course, many ways of preparing and eating commercial garden strawberries either as a dessert or cooked in the form of jams, puddings or tarts. The wild strawberry is a bit different, being smaller, with a flavour that, while sweet, is not as overpowering as that of the commercial varieties.

The fruit ripens in the mid-summer but obtaining a decent quantity requires careful searching. Once washed and de-stalked, these may be treated in the same manner as normal strawberries, and eaten raw with cream, added to a fruit salad or summer pudding, or boiled with sugar to form a jam. This is how they were consumed in historical times, with the main use being for desserts. Below I reproduce a 1759 recipe for strawberry fritters, a dish that remained popular into Victorian times.

*STRAWBERRY FRITTERS (1759 recipe)*
Make a paste with some flour, a spoonful of brandy, a glass of white wine, and the whites of two eggs, beat it up stiff, with some lemon-peel shred fine. Mix it well, not too thick or thin; then dip some strawberries into it and fry them.

*Historical Uses:* Strawberries are best known as a sweet fruit but herbalists have ascribed many medical properties to them when eaten fresh or in the form of a syrup. Their

*Wild strawberry (p. 73).*

*Wintercress (opposite).*

particular use was for dental conditions such as plaque, gum disease and ulcers. Other ascribed uses include an ability to reduce the symptoms of gout and chilblains and as an aid to kidney infections and high fevers. The nineteenth-century herbalist Constantine Rafinesque cautioned against over-indulging in this fruit as this would produce 'a painful stricture in the bladder, with red urine, as I have experienced myself'.

*Scientific Notes:* All the varieties and species of strawberry plant belong to the rose family (Rosaceae). Recent laboratory tests on extracts of wild strawberry have discovered that it contains active polyphenolic compounds which were observed to be effective at dilating blood vessels. This property is similar to the cardiovascular effects caused by extracts from hawthorn leaves and has drawn the interest of cardiologists.

## Wintercress – *Barbarea vulgaris*

> 'The taste of this herb, though ever so young, is bitterish, slimy and very nauseous; yet Linnaeus says it is used as a spring salad.'
>
> James Smith, 1801

- Alternative Names: Upland Cress, Yellow Rocket, Winter Rocket
- Etymology: Named after St Barbara
- Perennial; found in damp places across the British Isles but is more common in the south. Yellow flowers arranged in heads.

Despite the above low opinion of wintercress given by James Smith (which he repeats in several of his botanical works), this plant was at one time cultivated in gardens for use as a salad herb during the late winter and early spring, when other legumes were in short supply. The leaves taste bitter and should be picked before the late spring, when the plant flowers. There has been concern regarding the ability of wintercress to absorb and retain pesticides and other contaminants so do not forage from plants growing by the roadside, along the edges of fields or close to potential sources of pollution.

*Cookery:* There are mixed views concerning the culinary merits of wintercress, it possessing a somewhat harsh and bitter taste, especially when consumed raw. Wintercress leaves may be gathered in the late winter and early spring, when they are young and tender (but note the caution about contamination given above); they should be washed and then either chopped for use as a minor ingredient in salads or boiled/steamed for a few minutes and used as a vegetable side dish. Small quantities may also be added to light pasta or rice dishes in order to add a certain bite to the flavour.

*Historical Uses:* The principal historical medical uses for wintercress were in disorders of the bladder and kidneys, such as urinary infections and various stones. It was also used to treat cases of scurvy and would be applied to ulcerated wounds as an antiseptic.

*Scientific Notes:* Wintercress is part of the cabbage family (Brassicaceae). The plant has not been investigated for any potential medical or pharmaceutical properties, but its resistance to flea beetles (a crop pest) has been studied and is thought to be due to a genetic adaptation.

## Cow Parsley – *Anthriscus sylvestris*

> 'It is very good for old people that are dull and without courage: it rejoiceth and comforteth the heart, and increaseth their strength.'
>
> John Gerard, 1597

- Alternative Names: Wild Chervil, Wild Beaked Parsley, Cow Weed, Keck
- Etymology: Greek, *anthriscus*, the old name for this plant
- Perennial; widespread on grassy banks and in meadows across Britain.

Cow parsley, or wild chervil, is a common hedgerow plant that will be recognised by those who are familiar with the British countryside. The stems are stout and usually stand proud above the mass of undergrowth on verges and hedgerows. The young flowers and leaves have a mildly bitter (almost bland) taste and should be picked during spring, when tender.

WARNING. There are several similar-looking species including the infamous **highly poisonous plant hemlock** (*Conium maculatum*; see introductory section). Make sure of your identification and if you are in any doubt then do not attempt to eat. These plants are so similar that some historical botanists became confused and described cow parsley as being poisonous.

*Cookery:* In terms of culinary use, cow parsley has only a limited application. The young flowers and new leaves must be picked during the spring, otherwise they will be tough and inedible. The taste of this plant is so mild that it will become lost if used in soups or other recipes. Consequently it is best used raw and as such may be chopped and scattered across the top of salad dishes. It can also be steamed for a few minutes to provide a different, but inoffensive, garnish. In historical times the flowers and leaves would be bruised then infused into water for medical use or as a drink.

*Historical Uses:* British herbalists were fond of all the species of chervil and believed that they could aid digestion and promote general wellbeing. Of their properties, Nicholas Culpeper wrote: 'The root boiled, and eaten with oil and vinegar, (or without oil) does much please and warm old and cold stomachs oppressed with wind or phlegm, or those that have the consumption of the lungs. The same drank with wine is a preservation from the plague. It provoketh women's courses, and expelleth the after-birth, procureth an appetite to meat, and expelleth wind.' Quite an accomplishment for so common and humble a plant. It would also be mixed with fenugreek to treat skin conditions on sheep.

*Scientific Notes:* Cow parsley is part of the carrot family (Apiaceae). In common with some other closely related species, cow parsley contains deoxypodophyllotoxin, a compound which is being tested for possible anti-allergic properties. Similar compounds are currently used to relieve the symptoms of psoriasis, but it should be stressed that extracts from cow parsley have not yet been tested in this respect.

## Three-Cornered Garlic – *Allium triquetrum*

- Alternative Names: Three-edged Garlic, Three-stalked Garlic, Snow Bell, Onion Weed
- Etymology: Celtic, *all*, pungent
- Perennial; in fields and hedgerows of SW England. Locally common. White flowers, smells strongly of garlic.

Three-cornered garlic gains its name from its three-sided stem from which droop attractive bell-shaped white flowers. The plant may immediately be identified by the strong smell of garlic which it exudes on picking/bruising. It is an introduced plant from southern Europe which, according to one source, was first cultivated in the 1760s. It can only comfortably survive in south-western England and the Channel Islands and so gained little attention from botanists until the nineteenth century. Its leaves hold that unmistakable garlic smell and flavour. They may be picked during the spring for use as an herb.

*Cookery:* The fleshy leaves should be picked during early spring, at around the time that the plant's distinctive white flowers start to adorn grassy roadside verges. The leaves impart a strong garlic flavour and may be used as a substitute for traditional garlic bulbs in light dishes (such as soups) or as a garnish in soups and pasta dishes.

*Historical Uses:* There are no specific references to three-cornered garlic having been used in an historical medicinal capacity, probably because it is a relatively recent introduction to the British flora. Doubtless it would have been compared favourably to the more traditional garlic species (e.g. see ramsons).

*Scientific Notes:* All the species of garlic are members of the lily family (Lilaceae), which makes them close relations to the leeks, onions and tulips. Like other members of its genus, three-cornered garlic is a rich source of saponins, compounds which are often commercially promoted as having many health properties. However, clinical trials on saponins, including those extracted from three-cornered garlic, have thus far not produced any clear-cut medical benefits and there is the possibility that some of the compounds may be toxic in high doses.

Cow parsley (p. 76).

Three-cornered garlic (p. 77).

Sweet cicely (opposite).

## Sweet Cicely – *Myrrhis odorata*

'Sweet cicely has rather a sweet taste and a pleasant smell.'
Heinrich Link, 1822

- Alternative Name: Sweetsies
- Etymology: Greek, *murrha*, myrrh, from its fragrance
- Perennial; banks and grassy areas in northern England and Ireland, Wales and Scotland. White flowers, downy tri-pinnate leaves.

Sweet cicely is a rich, aromatic plant with a wonderful aniseed-like smell. It was at one time used to polish and perfume wooden floors in the north of England, a task for which it must have been well-suited. The leaves and flowers are picked in the spring.

WARNING: sweet cicely may be confused with the highly poisonous hemlock plant (*Conium maculatum*), so be absolutely certain of your identification before eating (see introductory section for more details).

*Cookery:* This plant is known for its sweet, aromatic taste which resembles that of fennel, an herb for which it would sometimes act as a substitute. In historical times the young leaves and seeds would be picked and roughly chopped for use as a flavouring in salads or as a general herb in stews and soups. There are historical sources which mention the leaves having been boiled and eaten as greens, but the flavour this imparts might be a little strong for the modern palate. In northern Europe sweet cicely seeds are used to flavour spirits, such as vodka and gin, including the famous Scandinavian alcoholic drink aquavit.

*Historical Uses:* Apothecaries ascribed the same medical properties to sweet cicely as to its close cousin, cow parsley (*q.v.*), with the additional ability to dissolve blood clots and reduce swellings. It was sometimes used in historical dentistry (often mixed in wine) as a disinfectant during surgery.

*Scientific Notes:* Sweet cicely is a member of the carrot family (Apiaceae) and is known to contain a variety of phenolic acids, some compounds of which have commercial and pharmacological uses, although the plant itself has not been clinically tested for any medical properties.

## Bistort – *Persicaria bistorta*

'Few indigenous vegetables possess greater astringency.'
Benjamin Barton, 1837

- Alternative Names: Adderwort, Dragonwort, Easter giant, Easter ledger, Easter ledges, Easter mangiant, Easter man-giant, Gentle dock, Great bistort, Osterick, Oysterloit, Passion dock, Patient dock, Pink pokers, Pudding grass, Pudding dock, Red legs, Snakeweed, Twice-writhen, Water ledges
- Etymology: Latin *persicarius*, a peach, because of the leaf shape
- Perennial; damp banks and meadows across Britain; localised and rarer in south. Flowers pink, in tall spikes; oval-shaped leaves.

Bistort is a distinctive and attractive plant that has been valued for its medicinal and edible qualities for centuries, especially in the north of Britain, where it is generally more commonly found. The young leaves and shoots have a rough, astringent taste and are generally foraged for during the spring.

*Cookery:* The use of bistort in culinary terms was at one time widespread, especially in northern England, when the young leaves would be added to puddings or boiled up as greens. The root tastes very bitter but would sometimes be dried, powdered and used to make bread. This tradition had all but ceased by Victorian times and I can find no historical recipe which specifically recommends the use of bistort as a cooking ingredient.

In general terms the young leaves and shoots should be picked and eaten in the spring, before the plant starts to flower in May/June. These may be boiled or steamed to form a vegetable side dish, or used as a general ingredient within a soup. Along with tansy pudding (*q.v.*), bistort would sometimes be eaten as a Lent dish, the chopped young leaves being beaten with eggs, flour and milk to form a pancake or omelette. This is perhaps why one of the many vernacular names afforded to this plant is 'Easter giant'.

*Historical Uses:* It was the root of bistort which the herbalists valued and such would be administered in cases of internal bleeding, dysentery, mouth ulcers and incontinence. Other uses include as a relief from smallpox, measles, venereal diseases, excessive menstruation and vomiting. In most cases the fresh root would be bruised and mixed with water. The leaves and flowers would sometimes be applied raw (or mixed with water) to stings and bites by venomous creatures.

*Scientific Notes:* Bistort is a member of the knotweed family (Polygonaceae). The plant's leaves contain concentrations of flavonoid compounds but the plant has not been scientifically assessed for any health-giving properties.

## Blackberries – *Rubus fructicosus*

> 'Many a poor village housewife brings a smile to the children's faces as she places her blackberry pie or pudding on the table, for it is a fruit that requires but little sugar, and is a cheap luxury added to the usual scanty meal.'
>
> Robert Chambers, 1832

- Etymology: Celtic, *reub*, to tear, because of its thorns
- Shrub; found in hedgerows, coppices and waste ground across all Britain. White flowers, long trailing stems with numerous small thorns.

The blackberry is a sweet, delicious autumn hedgerow fruit that was well known to the ancient Romans and Greeks, with Pliny considering them to be 'the food of man'. The fruit grows on the trailing, prickly bramble plant and has been the subject of foraging by young and old, rich and poor, for millennia. Even in these days of convenience food, blackberry-picking remains a common autumn pastime with the best spots being watched carefully until the fruit are deemed ripe enough to harvest. In times gone by there could be quite a scramble for the best blackberry locations, with those arriving too late finding themselves disappointed.

*Cookery:* Once picked, the blackberry has many potential uses. The Victorian writer 'Old Humphrey' (a pseudonym for George Mogridge) commented that: 'The blackberry is good, eat it how you will. It is good cooked or uncooked, in a pudding or a pie, plucked from the bush, or picked from the basket.'

The American cookery expert William Alcott agreed. In 1838 he wrote that: 'The blackberry forms a most delicious and nutritive breakfast now and then, for those who possess a pure taste; and if it is a little more astringent than the strawberry, it is nearly as wholesome.'

The quality and quantity of fruit on the bramble plant varies from year to year and is dependent on the weather with moderate summers generally resulting in the best crop. Pick blackberries which are black or purple in colour and soft to the touch (they come away from the plant without the need to tug); you will need about 400–500 grams to produce a decent-sized family pudding.

Once picked, the blackberries should be washed and drained. They may be eaten raw as a snack or dessert or used in a dish as a principal ingredient or perhaps in combination with other autumn fruits such as apples, raspberries, gooseberries and cherries. There are many recipes available, but here I present two that are based on traditional dishes.

*BLACKBERRY JAM*

Place 1 kilo of blackberries in a heavy saucepan with 120ml water and the juice of half a lemon. Bring to the boil and simmer for 30–40 mins or until the blackberries have become soft and pulpy. Add 1 kilo of jam-maker's sugar (the one with added pectin) or

*Bistort (p. 80).*

*Blackberries (p. 81).*

*Good king Henry (opposite).*

granulated sugar and the rind of a lemon. Boil rapidly for several minutes until the setting point is reached (see Preparation Technique for details of this). Ladle into clean jam jars, seal and label.

To make blackberry jelly, take the boiled blackberries and strain using a muslin bag (this will take several hours). Measure the resultant liquid and for every litre add 670g of jam-maker's sugar (see above), then follow directions as above.

*BLACKBERRY BRANDY (1832 recipe)*

Take the ripest blackberries. Mash them, put them in a linen bag and squeeze out the juice. To every quart (1.1 litres) of juice allow a pound (450g) of beaten loaf-sugar. Put the sugar into a large preserving kettle, and pour the juice on it. When it is all melted, set it on the fire, and boil it to a thin jelly. When cold, to every quart (1.1 litres) of juice allow a quart (1.1 litres) of brandy. Stir them well together, and bottle it for use. It will be ready to drink at once.

*Historical Uses:* The Romans believed that blackberry juice could be used to cure diseases of the mouth and throat, such as tonsillitis, and bramble roots, if dug up and boiled, were said to cure the dropsy (oedema). Other more general uses include as a soother of cold symptoms and a remedy against ringworm and snake bites. It used to be believed that the blackberries growing at the very top of a large bramble bush were unpalatable or even poisonous, but this is an old wives' tale.

*Scientific Notes:* The bramble plant (of which there are several varieties/subspecies) is part of the rose family (Rosaceae) and is closely related to the raspberry. Blackberries are naturally rich in fibre, natural sugars, vitamins C and K and several other essential minerals including manganese and folic acid. The berries have been measured to contain noticeable levels of enterolactone, a lignan compound that has been tentatively implicated in protection against certain types of cancer (e.g. prostate), although some clinical studies have found no proof for this.

## Good King Henry – *Chenopodium bonus-henricus*

> 'This plant is cultivated like spinach by the poorer class of people in Lincolnshire [and] eaten as substitutes for asparagus.'
>
> William Salisbury, 1816

- Alternative Names: Mercury Goosefoot, Lincolnshire Spinach
- Etymology: Greek, *chen*, a goose, and *pous*, a foot
- Perennial; local in meadows and fields; all Britain except far north. Green flowers on spikes, triangular leaves.

Good king Henry is part of the extensive goosefoot group of plants and was at one time cultivated as a domestic vegetable, it being prepared and eaten in much the same manner as spinach. The young shoots and leaves resemble spinach in taste but are perhaps more refined; they should be picked during the spring and summer. It should be noted that good king Henry is listed as being vulnerable in the wild so please take particular care when foraging for this plant.

*Cookery:* In general terms good king Henry should be foraged for its young shoots which may be cut from about April to June, and thereafter for its leaves which may be picked until the late summer.

If cut early enough, the shoots can be washed then steamed until tender and served with melted butter, just like asparagus. The leaves should be washed, then chopped and boiled or steamed to make a green vegetable side dish to accompany meat or fish dishes. When finely chopped, the leaves and shoots can be used as the principal ingredient in a soup or as a minor part of modern dishes such as stir-fries and risottos.

*Historical Uses:* The medicinal properties afforded to this plant by herbalists and apothecaries are relatively few, although I have seen it listed as part of a general cure for 'sudden fits and hysterical conditions'.

*Scientific Notes:* Good king Henry is one of several edible species from the goosefoot family (Chenopodiaceae). It does not seem to have been subject to any scrutiny with regard to its potential medicinal properties although, like similar species, it probably has high levels of oxalic acid (see entry for 'fat hen').

## Fat Hen – *Chenopodium album*

'It is generally esteemed a useless weed.'

James Smith, 1803

- Alternative Names: White Goosefoot, Lamb's Quarters, Wild Orache, Dungweed
- Etymology: Greek, *chen*, a goose, and *pous*, a foot
- Annual; fallow fields and waste ground across all of Britain.

In modern gardens and farms, fat hen (a name which is said to have originated in Norfolk) is regarded as something of a nuisance, it being quick to colonise disturbed ground such as ploughed fields and flower-beds. In past centuries it was particularly associated with dunghills, a habit which led to it being called 'dungweed' in parts of England.

As an edible plant, fat hen was not disliked by everyone and there is evidence that it may have been cultivated as a food source in prehistoric times (its fossilised remains having been found on archaeological sites). In the current day it is still grown as a subsistence crop in parts of Africa. Everything written here about fat hen may be applied to its close relation red goosefoot (*Chenopodium rubrum*) which may be found in similar conditions and is prepared and eaten in the same way.

*Cookery:* The plant is tall and distinctive and is noted by several early nineteenth-century botanists to have at one time been widely eaten in Britain, although they inevitably speak of this in the past tense, suggesting that the practice had died out by the 1840s.

No historical recipes are given other than to say that the leaves and young shoots would be picked during the spring and summer, boiled and eaten as greens, often in the place of spinach. In fact, fat hen may be prepared and eaten in the same manner as its close relation, good king Henry (*q.v.*). In this respect, the young shoots may be steamed and eaten with butter, while the leaves should be boiled/steamed and served as greens. It is said that the Germans would gather the seeds (which are black and plentiful) and either grind them for use in bread dough or boil them as a side dish.

*Historical Uses:* Fat hen does not seem to have been ascribed any specific medicinal properties by herbalists, but is sometimes lumped together with good king Henry and other members of the goosefoot family.

*Scientific Notes:* Fat hen is one of several closely related species from the goosefoot family (Chenopodiaceae). The seeds and leaves of fat hen are high in fibre, vitamin A and potassium but also contain significant levels of oxalic acid, a substance that, if consumed excessively, may lead to crystalline deposits in the kidney (kidney stones) and gut.

## Mugwort – *Artemisia vulgaris*

'Mugwort are put upon the doors and over the roofs of their houses.'
John Pinkerton, 1811

- Alternative Names: Common Wormwood, St John's Girdle
- Etymology: Latin, *Artemisia*, the old name for the plant
- Perennial; not uncommon in hedgerows and verges; rarer in northern Britain than in the south. Woolly leaves, green above, white beneath.

During more superstitious times mugwort was placed about houses to keep out the Devil, in much the same way that garlic is said to ward off vampires. The plant is weakly aromatic, geographically widespread and has been used ritually in many parts of the world, especially in eastern Asia. It has a bitter taste which does not suit everyone and the leaves are best picked during the spring and early summer. Raw mugwort has mild hallucinogenic properties which are destroyed on cooking: it is not recommended for pregnant women.

*Cookery:* Mugwort leaves should be picked during the spring or early summer before the plant flowers (normally around midsummer). They are quite bitter and although the plant is incorporated into ceremonial food in the Far East, it is probably too astringent for use as a main cooking ingredient.

In Europe mugwort has traditionally been used as an herb for flavouring roast meat dishes in much the same way as rosemary. A sprig of mugwort placed inside a roast chicken will flavour the meat but it may also be used for a variety of other oven-roast meats such as lamb and even fish. A second use for mugwort is as an herbal infusion, for which a few leaves may be placed in a cup with boiling water. The leaves have also been used during the fermentation of beer to enhance the bitter flavour of hops.

*Historical Uses:* The most common historical use of mugwort was as an insect repellent, in which capacity it would often be grown in gardens or placed in strategic positions around the house. Traditional herbalist works mention that mugwort flowers could be used as an aid to childbirth and that it was generally helpful for people suffering from hysterical fits. It would generally be administered in the form of a tea or warm bath, but it has been suggested that women suffering from menstrual cramps could sit on boiled mugwort leaves. The leaves were also said to have been used to ease powder burns and gunshot wounds during the English Civil War. The medical virtues of mugwort were

Fat hen (p. 84).

Mugwort (p. 85).

Mugwort tea (p. 85).

Medlar fruit (p. 88).

Medlars after harvesting.

*Silverweed (p. 89).*

*Silverweed leaves.*

played down during the early nineteenth century and afterwards the plant was mostly excluded from serious medical textbooks, although it is still used by some modern alternative practitioners.

*Scientific Notes:* Mugwort is part of the daisy family (Asteraceae). The plant contains a chemical called thujone which is thought to act on the brain in a similar manner to cannabis. Thujone is being investigated for potential medicinal uses, including as an antidote to certain opiates. Mugwort is known to trigger hay fever and other allergic reactions and this is thought to be especially severe in those that suffer from sensitivity to peaches.

## Medlar – *Mespilus germanica*

> 'The tree is cultivated for the use of the fruit, which have the appearance of small rotten apples.'
>
> Nicholas Culpeper, 1652

- Etymology: Greek, *Mespilus*, the old name for the plant
- Tree; mostly cultivated in gardens and orchards but is semi-naturalised in some southern English woodlands. White flowers, thorny branches with lanceolate leaves.

During Victorian times medlar trees were widely cultivated for their distinctive fruit which would commonly be turned into a rich jelly to be eaten with cheese. These days the medlar tree is a rare sight and will generally only be found in well-established gardens and orchards, although semi-naturalised examples will sometimes be found in old hedgerows and woodlands in southern England. The fruit appears in the autumn but should not be picked until after the first frosts have occurred. Its taste is hard to describe but it certainly has elements of apple in it, perhaps with a hint of fig.

*Cookery:* Medlar fruit resemble small apples but they are very hard and so must be 'bletted' before being picked. In effect this means waiting for the first winter frosts to attack the fruit, after which the skin will turn brown and wrinkly and the flesh soften. Historically, this process would be accomplished at home by placing the fruit in boxes of straw and then leaving them to ripen naturally for a couple of weeks in a dark, dry place. In the modern household the bletting process may be speeded up by placing the fruit overnight in the freezer and then storing them until very ripe.

In Victorian times the ripe (some would say rotten) flesh of the medlar fruit would be scooped out and eaten raw or as an accompaniment to cheese, but it works just as well with vanilla ice cream or just plain cream and sugar.

A more traditional use for medlar is as the ingredient for a jelly which would be made and eaten in much the same manner as apple jelly and was especially popular as an accompaniment to meat dishes such as pork. A historical recipe for medlar jelly is given below but given the current rarity of this fruit, it is possible to use cooking apples as a partial substitute. A stiffer, more viscous, version of this jelly would sometimes be poured into moulds and served under the title of medlar cheese.

*MEDLAR JELLY (based on a 1798 recipe)*
Take 500g of ripe medlars and place in a heavy pan with about 200ml of water and the rind of a lemon. Bring to the boil, cover, then simmer until soft and pulpy. Strain through a muslin bag into a bowl (this may take several hours). Measure the resultant liquid and place in a heavy pan; for every 500ml of liquid, add 330g of sugar and the juice from one lemon. Warm until the sugar dissolves, then boil vigorously for 10–15 mins, removing any surface scum, until the setting point is reached (see Preparation Technique for details of this). Place in clean jam jars and seal at once. You can bulk out/alter the flavour of this recipe by adding cooking apples.

*Historical Uses:* Extract of the medlar fruit was traditionally associated with pregnancy and childbirth, it being said to help allay the possibility of miscarriage and to alleviate morning sickness, cravings and post-natal depression. Its other main use was as a dressing for open wounds and sores and as a mouthwash for those with sore throats and ulcers.

*Scientific Notes:* The medlar tree is part of the rose family (Rosaceae). Several studies have looked at the chemical changes that occur in medlar fruit as they ripen on the tree but the results were not unexpected, revealing progressive changes in various sugars and enzymes. Older studies suggest that the fruit may have a beneficial effect on the cardiovascular system, although this has not been established with certainty.

## Silverweed – *Argentina anserina*

> 'Now Dame Venus hath fitted women with two herbs of one name, one to help conception, the other to maintain beauty, and what more can be expected of her?'
>
> Nicholas Culpeper, 1652

- Alternative Name: Silverweed Cinquefoil
- Etymology: Latin, *argentums*, silver, from the hue of its leaves
- Perennial; grassy verges around all of Britain. Yellow flowers, leaves highly serrated with a silvery appearance.

Silverweed gains its name from the silky, silvery shine that adorns its leaves and which, together with its bright yellow flower, makes it a highly attractive plant. The roots of this plant are said to have been an important and widely used food source in the Middle Ages, especially in northern England and Scotland where the plant may even have been cultivated. However, the culinary attractions of the plant did not survive into the modern era, it perhaps being supplanted by more domesticated root vegetables such as parsnips, carrots and potatoes. Forage for the root during the summer and autumn (but see the introductory section regarding the legality of uprooting wild plants).

*Cookery:* It is the roots of silverweed that are edible, having a sort of nutty, starchy taste that some compare to parsnips although I don't think this is an exact description. The roots are traditionally foraged for during the summer and autumn, then boiled and eaten like carrots. This practice is said to have been widespread in medieval times, especially in northern England and Scotland, but after the eighteenth century there is little mention of people having used this plant as a staple food source.

Silverweed roots are quite thin and straggly and may extend for some distance from the plant, making it necessary to dig two or more plants for a decent meal. Thoroughly clean the roots of soil and then scrape off the rough skin. The roots may then be steamed, boiled or roasted and eaten (with butter) as an accompaniment to Sunday lunch.

Historically the roots would also be dried out and then ground into a powder which was used as a general additive for soups and other dishes. The leaves, while not eaten directly, have been used to create silverweed wine and tea.

*Historical Uses:* The earlier quote by Nicholas Culpeper refers to two plants, tansy (for use in pregnancy) and silverweed, which was commonly used as a cosmetic. Indeed, the main use of silverweed to herbalists was as a skin improver, it being said to lessen blemishes, remove freckles and prevent blisters if placed in the shoes. It was frequently used as a treatment for wounds and toothache and as a cure for stomach upsets. It was generally extracts of the roots that were harvested for this purpose, they being either dried and then powdered or bruised and infused in water, oil or vinegar.

*Scientific Notes:* Silverweed is a member of the rose family (Rosaceae). It does not appear to have been subject to any formal scientific analysis or clinical trials.

*Chapter Three*

# Woodlands and Forests

The woodland and forest areas of Britain are mostly of small extent and relatively recent origin, especially when compared to those found in Europe and America. Many British woodlands were long ago cut down to meet the demands of farming, industry and householders, leaving very few untouched patches of forest, most of which are to be found in remote parts of Scotland. Much of this initial destruction took place centuries ago during the Bronze and Iron Ages but the process has been repeated many times since: the need for wood and cleared land for farming or development will always take priority over the natural beauty of the forest.

*The magic of Britain's woodlands.*

The relative modernity of British woodlands does not stop them from being a wonderful asset to our wildlife and there are few more pleasurable pastimes than a walk through a stretch of woodland. Dappled sunlight filtering through a canopy of fresh spring leaves is entrancing but even in the depths of the worst winter, these places can be magical. It is no wonder that so many of our playwrights and novelists have endowed the forest with supernatural qualities and fantastical creatures such as fairies, fawns and witches.

Many woodlands are dominated by trees and large bushes with only a minimal amount of undergrowth. This makes them wonderful places to forage for fruits, nuts and berries but you will often be in competition with other animals such as squirrels, birds and deer. Beneath the leafy canopy light and rain are usually at a premium and so the undergrowth is often restricted to a few hardy plants, some of which are edible. However, in open woodlands and on the edge of forests, there may be a rich undergrowth akin to that found on verges or in hedgerows: thus many of the species found in this situation are covered in Chapter Two.

The best woodlands and forests are those with deciduous trees that grow in lowland areas and valleys. Pine forests, and especially plantations, often grow on thin, acidic soils and do not favour a diversity of tree species, especially in mountain regions. Nor do they encourage a dense undergrowth of smaller plants. That said, it is usually possible to find something edible, even in the most apparently inhospitable of places, so do not be put off from looking.

Woodlands are in general less prone to some of the pollution issues that affect more accessible regions (e.g. weedkillers and car fumes) but take the usual precautions anyway (see introductory chapter). It is surprisingly easy to become disorientated and lost inside even quite small stretches of woodland, so it may be best to take a decent map with you as well as a compass or GPS (although the latter may not work in dense woods). When moving about (and especially if you leave well-trodden paths) watch out for slippery surfaces, wasps' nests, rotten logs, tree roots and dog dirt.

## Common Ash Tree – *Fraxinus excelsior*

> 'Singularly good against the bitings of the viper, adder or any other venomous beast.'
>
> Nicholas Culpeper, 1652

- Etymology: Latin, *frango*, to split, because of the properties of its wood
- Common across the British Isles, including in parks and town centres.

There are several species of ash tree found in Britain but most are restricted to parks and gardens. It is just the native common ash that will be found growing wild in hedgerows, woodlands and coppices across the countryside. Its distinctive seeds are edible and have a bitter, astringent taste that lends itself to pickling. Harvests of the seeds may be varied with some years being abundant, others very poor.

*Cookery:* It is the paddle-shaped seeds of the tree that are used in cookery. They are traditionally called 'ash keys' or, in some parts, 'kitty-keys', and should be picked when very young and green. If you wait too long then the keys become tough and unpalatable.

Ash keys should be steeped in vinegar (see recipe below) to produce an aromatic but bitter-tasting pickle for use as a condiment with meat dishes. One historical source recommends mixing fresh ash keys directly with salt and vinegar, then immediately using them as 'delicate salading sauce'. However, the keys will benefit from several weeks' pickling before being served.

*PICKLED ASH KEYS (1737 recipe)*

Having those [ash keys] which are young, plump and very tender, parboil them in a little fair water, then take a pint of white wine, half a pint (285ml) of vinegar, the juice of a couple of lemons, and a little salt, and boil them together. Let it stand by 'till it is cold, then put in the ash keys into the pickle, and cover them.

Modern recipes differ little from this except that it is considered better to boil the keys in two changes of water (this removes some of the bitterness) before straining and placing them in pickling jars. Take approximately 500ml of either white wine vinegar or cider vinegar and warm in a pan. Add a couple of tablespoons of brown sugar, some peppercorns, salt and cloves, and heat gently until bubbles start to appear. Strain through a sieve and place in the pickling jar with the keys. Seal and leave to mature for at least eight weeks. The keys may also be used to make a bitter but drinkable herbal tea.

*Historical Uses:* Ancient folklore dictated that the ash tree was so disliked by vipers that, when confronted with their leaves, they would turn and flee, even if it meant passing through a fire to do so. Nicholas Culpeper was sceptical of this but did believe that ash leaves and bark, if digested or applied externally, were 'singularly good against the bitings of the viper, adder or any other venomous beast'. Other herbalist uses included parts of the ash as a cure for skin burns, scabs and leprosy as well as for stitches, jaundice and flatulence.

*Scientific Notes:* The ash tree is part of the olive family (Oleaceae) which includes familiar shrubs such as lilac and jasmine. Extracts from the ash tree have been observed to have anti-inflammatory properties during laboratory trials and it is speculated that there may be applications with regard to arthritis. Other studies reveal the plant to have diuretic properties and that it might induce hypertension.

*Ash keys (p. 92).*

*Beech nuts (opposite).*

## Beech Tree – *Fagus sylvatica*

'The nuts do much nourish such beasts as feed thereon.'
Nicholas Culpeper, 1652

- Etymology: Greek, *phago*, to eat, because of its nuts
- Common on chalky ground in England and Wales.

Beech trees are a graceful and enchanting feature of the English landscape (they are rarer in Scotland) where they are especially associated with the thin chalky soils of the downs. It is the tree's fruit, the beech nut, that is eaten but humans must compete for them with a variety of woodland animals and especially squirrels. This makes finding ripe nuts difficult. In times past beech trees would be commercially harvested with the nuts being sold at markets or used to feed pigs.

*Cookery:* The most palatable part of the beech tree is the beech nut (sometimes called beech masts) which may be harvested as windfalls from the ground or direct from the tree from late summer onwards. The fruit is encased in a soft shell which turns brown and opens when ripe, at which point they may be peeled away by hand. The nuts themselves do not preserve well and should be roasted or cooked relatively soon after picking. The nuts may be roasted in a medium oven or under the grill and then salted to make a tasty snack, although one 1802 cookery book cautions that eaten in excess 'they occasion giddiness and headache'. There are references to the nuts being dried and ground for use as bread flour.

The beech nut abounds with oil which may be extracted easily by macerating the nuts using a pestle and mortar or electric grinder, then squeezing the pulp through a fine sieve or muslin bag. The oil, which is yellow and more commonly used in France than the British Isles, has several domestic applications, including as a cooking oil which can operate at a high temperature, as well as being a substitute for olive oil in salad dressings. The production of beech nut oil was once a commercial affair but by mid-Victorian times it was found 'to be more profitable to fatten the swine upon the nuts'.

*Historical Uses:* Apothecaries did not much use the tree but the leaves are said to reduce swellings when applied to the skin, while the water that accumulates in the tree's hollows 'will cure both man and beast of any scurf, scab or running tetters'.

*Scientific Notes:* The beech tree is part of the chestnut family (Fagaceae). Beech nuts are high in protein but they do not seem to have attracted the attention of the scientific community, although it has been suggested that the oil could have potential as a biofuel.

## **Sweet Chestnut – *Castanea sativa***

> 'Chestnuts form a wholesome and grateful food to many quadrupeds, as well as to mankind.'
>
> James Smith, 1812

- Alternative Name: Spanish Chestnut
- Etymology: Latin, *castanea*, old name for this tree
- Very common in a wide variety of situations, from woodlands to roadsides and parks. Most common in southern Britain.

The brown, rounded form of the fruit from the sweet chestnut tree will be familiar to most readers (as will their prickly yellow husks) and, despite our reliance on supermarkets, that practice of gathering the autumn windfalls remains commonplace. The sweet chestnut tree is not native to the British Isles and is thought to have been introduced by the Romans, probably as a food source. The historical and modern popularity of the sweet chestnut is a testament both to its sweet, nutty taste and to its versatility, it having being used for a variety of purposes, including as a stuffing for poultry. The chestnuts may be foraged on the ground during the early autumn.

*Cookery:* It is possible to buy chestnuts at the supermarket but given their abundance in the wild, there is no real need to do so. Simply find a sweet chestnut tree (not to be confused with the inedible horse chestnut or conker tree) and keep an eye on it until the distinctive globular, yellow, prickly husks begin to drop off in the early weeks of autumn. The brown sweet chestnuts lie within these spiky balls and will often tumble out onto the ground. Each spiky ball will contain two or three nuts, but only select the plumpest ones (leave the smaller chestnuts for squirrels and other animals). I suggest using gloves to extract them, although one can also roll the spiky chestnut casing gently under a shoe to force the nuts out.

Chestnuts are inedible raw and so must be cooked to release their flavour. There are two options for this but in either case first use a knife to cut a cross shape at the top of each chestnut to prevent them from exploding. (1) roast them, either on an open fire, or in a hot oven, until the shells have split; or (2) blanch them by placing them in boiling water for a few minutes to soften the skins, then remove the skin and continue boiling until tender. In both instances, the chestnuts should be eaten or used in further recipes soon afterwards as they do not hold their flavour for long.

*CHESTNUT PURÉE (1832 recipe)*

Into two cups (560ml) of boiling milk place one pound (450g) of shelled chestnuts and cook until tender. Then mash, strain and season with salt, pepper and butter. This may be eaten as a side vegetable but it is also a splendid accompaniment to poached eggs.

*CHESTNUT AND CELERY SOUP (based on an 1829 recipe)*
Blanch 500g of chestnuts and remove their skins. Cut up a large onion and fry in oil until light brown, add the chestnuts and cut up six stalks of celery. Add 1 litre of vegetable stock and cook for half an hour or until the celery is tender. Take off the heat, slowly stir in 200ml of milk and continue to cook for a few minutes. Then use a blender to purée the mixture and continue cooking until the desired thickness is reached (add more stock, if necessary).

*CHESTNUT COMPOTE (1832 recipe)*
Roast your chestnuts and when they are peeled and skinned, put them into a saucepan, with a quarter of a pound (115g) of sugar, and half a glass of water. Let them simmer for a quarter of an hour. Squeeze in a little lemon juice, and when ready to serve, strew caster sugar over them.

*CHESTNUT CUSTARD (1832 recipe)*
Take three pounds (1350g) of well roasted chestnuts, removing such parts as were coloured by the fire, and pound them with a pound (450g) of fresh butter. When a smooth paste, add three-quarters of a pound (340g) of caster sugar, the yolks of twelve eggs, a pinch of salt, and a few spoonfuls of whipped cream, the whites whipped firm, and finish the custard as directed.

*Historical Uses:* Strangely, apothecaries did not think much of the sweet chestnut, although they do ascribe curative properties to its unpalatable (but only distantly related) namesake, the horse chestnut.

*Scientific Notes:* The sweet chestnut tree is part of the beech family (Fagaceae). Extracts from sweet chestnut leaves have been shown to have antibacterial properties and to contain significant quantities of antioxidants.

## Crab Apple – *Malus sylvestris*

'When all aloud the wind doth blow,
And coughing drowns the parson's saw,
And birds sit brooding in the snow,
And Marian's nose looks red and raw,
When roasted crabs hiss in the bowl,
Then nightly sings the staring owl:
Tu-whit, tu-whoo!'

Shakespeare, *Love's Labour's Lost*

- Alternative Name: Wild Apple
- Etymology: Latin, *malus*, bad
- Occasional in woodlands and hedgerows across Britain.

Sweet chestnuts (p. 96).

Crab apples (p. 97 and opposite).

Historically known as the wild apple, this tree was once a frequent sight in copses and hedgerows across Britain and, although rarer these days, it may still be found with a little searching. (NB some hedgerow apple trees are naturalised from orchards; their blossom tends to be more pink than that of the crab apple.) The origin of the name is uncertain; some sources claim it from the Norse word for a wild apple *skrabba*, while others believe it is a description of the astringent taste. The crab apple tree produces a mass of white/light pink flowers in late May and its small, globular fruit in the early autumn.

*Cookery:* Unlike the cultivated eating apple, fruit from the crab apple tree has a decidedly sour taste, but this has not stopped it from being a popular fruit since at least Neolithic times. The two commonest modern uses for the crab apple are to make a sweet jelly preserve and in the fermentation of wine.

*CRAB APPLE JELLY*

Quarter the fruit and remove any black spots. Place into a pan with a little water to prevent burning and boil, adding more water as necessary. When the apples have turned into a pulp, place in a straining bag and drain off the juice into a bowl (this may take some hours). For each pint (560ml) of crab apple juice, place a pound and a quarter (570g) of sugar into a heavy pan; pour the juice over this and stir it in, heating gently if necessary. Boil vigorously for around 20 mins, removing any surface scum. Test for the setting point (see Preparation Technique for details of this). Pour it into clean jam jars and seal immediately. Unopened it will keep for several months.

*CRAB APPLE POSTILLA (1822 recipe)*

Bake the crab apples in an oven then pulp through a sieve. Sweeten with sugar or honey, and beating up the mixture with a wooden spoon till it is all of a froth. Then put on two trays, and bake for two hours in an oven moderately hot. After this another layer of the beaten apples is added, and pounded loaf sugar [i.e. granulated sugar] is spread over. Sometimes a still finer sort is made, by beating yolks of eggs to a froth, and then mixing it with the apple juice.

*Historical Uses:* The medical uses are few, although the leaves of the tree are said to help heal burns and wounds.

*Scientific Notes:* The crab apple tree is part of the broad rose family of plants (Rosaceae). Crab apples, while popular with horticulturalists, have not induced the pharmacological or scientific communities to study them.

## Ramsons – *Allium ursinum*

> 'The milk of cows that eat it becomes intolerably nauseous from the well-known garlic flavour.'
>
> Philip Miller, 1835

- Alternative Names: Wild Garlic, Bear's Garlic, Broad-leaved Garlic
- Etymology: Celtic, *all*, pungent, because of the scent
- Perennial; locally common in shady woodlands across the British Isles. White flowers, garlic smell, leaves radiate from root.

Immediately recognisable by its all-pervasive garlic smell, ramsons is a well-known plant that has been widely used in historical and modern cuisine. It is best looked for in damp, shady locations within woodlands and copses, where it may sometimes be abundant, but plants will also occur in hedges and on path verges. The leaves impart a mild but distinct garlic flavour and may be picked at any time.

*Cookery:* The leaves of ramsons should be harvested by careful cutting with a knife. Take the youngest leaves and do not denude the plant of all its foliage. They may then be used raw (but chopped) as a substitute for garlic or spring onions in salads, or as a garnish to soups, risotto, seafood and other light meals. The flavour is not as overpowering as the plant's smell might lead you to believe, and in many situations the leaves make a quick and convenient substitute for the fiddly garlic bulbs sold by supermarkets.

*Historical Uses:* In herbalist terms, the obvious garlic aroma and flavour of ramsons led to it being included with other such plants in this family including the familiar domestic garlic. As such it was said to be useful for diseases of the blood and lungs, but also as a highly effective prophylactic against a variety of diseases including influenza, smallpox and bubonic plague. In fact, there are probably very few ailments which have not at one time or another had garlic prescribed for them and even today it is available from chemists and health food shops in the form of capsules.

*Scientific Notes:* Like other garlic plants, ramsons is part of the lily family (Liliaceae). Laboratory trials suggest that ransoms may have beneficial protective effects on the cardiovascular system. Like other members of the garlic family, ransoms contains high levels of flavonoids, some of which are believed to have a thinning effect on the blood.

## Elder Tree – *Sambucus nigra*

> 'Elder is a whole magazine of physic to rustic practitioners, nor is it quite neglected by more regular ones.'
>
> James Smith, 1801

- Alternative Names: Black Elder, Elderberry Tree
- Etymology: Greek, *sambuke*, a musical instrument
- Tree; common in woodlands and hedgerows across the British Isles. Produces clusters of white, sweet-scented flowers.

One of the delights of the late spring and early summer is the sight of elder trees laden with dozens of white flower heads, all of which impart a sweet, intoxicating scent. The elder is my family's favourite edible plant and each spring my daughter and I gather handfuls of the flower heads in order to create a delicious, refreshing elderflower drink. I head back to the same trees in the autumn when they produce clusters of small black berries. The sweet, edible delight of the elder tree has been known about for millennia but do not be tempted to eat the berries raw as they will upset your stomach; also, some people have a mild allergic reaction to the flowers.

*Cookery:* The two main components of the elder tree are its flowers and berries, which respectively appear during late spring and early autumn. Historically the young shoots have also been harvested for use in pickles or as an alternative for celery but these should be avoided, given that the green parts of the tree are known to contain toxic chemicals.

The white, sweet-scented flowers should be gathered carefully so as not to disturb the loose pollen and should not be washed before use (they may, however, be dried for later use). The flowers may be used for a variety of cold and hot drinks as well as wine (see recipes below) but, because they should not be washed, it is necessary to sieve any elderflower-derived drinks through a very fine sieve or straining bag to remove any impurities, such as small insects. Alternatively, leave the drink to cool and settle overnight, then carefully siphon or pour the clear liquid away from the sediment.

The berries appear in early autumn and turn a dark purple or black colour when ripe; they should only be foraged for when ripe and should never, ever, be eaten raw. They are used as the prime ingredient within a variety of preserves including jams, jellies and chutneys, as well as for wine. The cooked berries may also be added to other fruits, such as blackberries and raspberries, for use in pies.

*ELDERFLOWER CORDIAL*

Place roughly ten flower heads (fresh or dried) into a large bowl and add boiling water from the kettle. Add about 800g of sugar, a whole lemon (sliced) and leave to one side for several hours. Strain the liquid through a very fine sieve (this removes insects and other

*Ramsons (p. 100).*

*Elder tree flowers (p. 101).*

debris trapped in the flowers) and bottle the resultant cordial. It will keep for several days in a fridge or, for longer storage, may be placed in the freezer (in a suitable container or as ice cubes). To taste the drink, dilute the cordial with tap (or sparkling) water; this produces a wonderful, refreshing summer drink. For elderflower tea, infuse the flowers in a pan of boiling water for 10 mins, then strain and drink hot or cold. Add sugar/a slice of lemon as desired.

*ELDERBERRY JELLY*
Take 1 kilo of washed, ripe elderberries and crush them in a bowl. Place in a heavy pan with a small amount of water and boil for several minutes, until pulped. Place in a muslin bag and strain into a large bowl (this will take several hours). Put the resultant liquid into a heavy pan and add 80ml of water, the rind and juice of two lemons and 550g of sugar. Boil vigorously for 10–20 mins (removing any surface scum with a slotted spoon) until the setting point is reached (see Preparation Technique for details of this). Pour the liquid into clean jars and seal immediately; it will keep for several months unopened.

*ELDERBERRY WINE (1833 recipe)*
To every quart (1.1 litres) of berries put two quarts (2.2 litres) of water, boil for half an hour, run the liquor and break the fruit through a fine sieve. Then to every quart (1.1 litres) of juice put three quarters of a pound (340g) of Lisbon sugar, coarse, but not the very coarsest. Boil the whole for a quarter of an hour, with some peppers, ginger, and a few cloves. Pour it into a tub, and when of a proper warmth, into the barrel, with toast and yeast to work. When it ceases to hiss, put a quart (1.1 litres) of brandy to eight gallons (4.5 litres), and stop up. Bottle in the spring or at Christmas. The liquor must be in a warm place to make it work.

*ELDERFLOWER WINE (1823 recipe)*
Boil eighteen pounds (8.1 kilos) of white powder-sugar, with six gallons (27 litres) of water, and two whites of eggs well beaten. Then skim it, and put in a quarter of a peck (2.2 litres) of elderflowers from the tree that bears white berries. Do not keep them on the fire. When near cold, stir it, and put in six spoonful of lemon-juice, four or five of yeast, and beat well into the liquor. Stir it every day. Put six pounds (2.7 kilos) of the best raisins, stoned, into the cask. Stop it close, and bottle in six months.

*Historical Uses:* Elder was not just popular for its edible qualities: it was also highly valued as a medicinal plant. The flowers would be infused in hot water and the drink used to calm people's nerves, while the berries would be turned into remedies for sore throats and chesty coughs (commercial versions of this are still available in some parts of Europe). The bark was also said to have laxative properties.

*Scientific Notes:* The elder tree is part of the honeysuckle family of plants (Caprifoliaceae). Extracts of elder have been tested for possible antiviral activity, including in relation to HIV, but with negative results.

## Hazel Tree – *Corylus avellana*

> 'If anything of the hazelnut be stopping, it is the husks and shells, and nobody be so mad as to eat them.'
>
> Nicholas Culpeper, 1652

- Etymology: Greek, *korus*, a cap
- Native tree; common in woods, hedgerows, coppices and gardens across the British Isles.

The hazel tree can be a prodigious producer of the familiar hazelnuts (also known as filberts), bags of which are sold in grocery stores during the late autumn and Christmas seasons. Hazelnuts are an ancient and much prized food source which, to judge by archaeological evidence, probably formed an important part of the diet of many prehistoric societies. The nuts are delicious, can be stored for lengthy periods and, while often eaten raw, are also used in a variety of recipes.

*Cookery:* Hazelnuts appear on the trees from August onwards but they do not ripen until the mid-autumn, after which time they may be picked or shaken (but not beaten) from the tree. The nuts are a sought-after commodity and there is often competition from other foragers and squirrels. The nuts are encased in a tough husk and so may be stored for many weeks in a cool place before opening. In historical times the nuts would be put in an earthenware pot and buried in sandy soil. Before eating, the husk must be removed with a nutcracker or similar implement.

Hazelnuts are a versatile food which has a variety of uses that includes eating them raw, chopping them for a garnish and roasting them. There are literally dozens of hazelnut recipes available in cookbooks but I have a simple and delicious way to eat them. Take the shelled nuts and place them on a baking tray in a hot oven; watch closely until the nuts start to turn brown (after about 10–15 mins). Remove from the oven and then fry in a saucepan of hot melted butter, coating them generously before serving as a mid-morning snack.

*HAZELNUT ICE (1827 recipe)*
Take a pound (450g) of hazelnuts, shell them, and caramelise them under the grill with half a pound of sugar. Put them on a leaf to cool. Break them in a mortar, and put them into eight yolks of eggs, and four pints (2.3 litres) of rich cream. Let them cook together with the eggs; rub them through a search, and ice [freeze] them.

*Historical Uses:* The hazelnut has had a mixed reputation among apothecaries. In the Middle Ages it was believed that excessive consumption of these nuts could cause constipation, dysentery and asthma. Thus few medicinal uses were ascribed to the tree, but later herbalist writers do mention that preparations based on the nuts are effective for easing the symptoms of coughs and for regulating the menstrual cycle.

*Scientific Notes:* The hazel tree is part of the birch family (Betulaceae). Extracts from hazel leaves have been shown to be high in antioxidants and have antimicrobial properties.

## Wood Avens – *Geum urbanum*

> 'The root in the springtime, when steeped in wine, doth give it a delicate savour and taste.'
>
> Nicholas Culpeper, 1652

- Alternative Names: Herb Bennett, Colewort, St Benedict's herb
- Etymology: Greek, *geuo*, a pleasant taste
- Perennial; common in woodlands and shaded hedgerows across the British Isles. Yellow, erect flowers.

Wood avens is a rather inconspicuous plant which produces an attractive yellow flower in the late spring and summer. In ancient times it was better known for its ascribed medical qualities than its culinary prowess, but the plant's roots are edible and have an aromatic flavour reminiscent of cloves. It should be harvested in the spring and summer.

*Cookery:* It is the thin, straggly roots that hold the plant's flavour; these should be harvested in the spring and summer and washed thoroughly before use (see Introduction regarding the uprooting of wild plants). They may be dried and stored over winter. Although not used as a major cooking ingredient, wood avens was often used to flavour wine and beer, either during the fermenting process or afterwards by adding the roots to wine casks.

The roots impart a similar taste and smell to that of cloves and may generally be used as a substitute for this spice in a variety of sweet and savoury dishes (such as apple desserts, Indian dishes, pickles, sauces, etc.). With most recipes the use of around eight to ten rootlets will replace the need for cloves; the roots themselves should be tied in a bunch and cooked with the food, then removed from the dish before serving.

*Historical Uses:* The roots of wood avens were afforded many curative properties, most of which concerned digestive disorders such as diarrhoea, heartburn, flatulence and stomach cramps. It was also said to be beneficial for liver and heart disorders, to act as an antidote to some poisons and to fend off the plague. Dried roots would be used to ward off insects and, if applied to the face, could cure acne.

*Scientific Notes:* Wood avens is part of the rose family (Rosaceae). Laboratory trials suggest that wood avens may have significant anti-inflammatory properties with regard to diseases and wounds but this has yet to be tested clinically.

Hazel tree nuts (p. 104).

Wood avens (p. 105).

Juniper berries (opposite).

## Juniper – *Juniperus communis*

> 'They have a warm pungent sweetish taste, which if they are long chewed, is followed by a considerable bitterness.'
>
> William Woodville, 1832

- Etymology: Latin, *juniperus*, old name of the plant
- Tree; common on hillsides, mountains and downs across the British Isles. Needle-like leaves, blue-black berries in small clusters.

Known since Biblical times, there are many different species of juniper tree worldwide, some of which can tolerate the extreme climatic conditions found in mountains and deserts. The common juniper of Britain forms dense bushes or small trees whose branches are laden with prickly needle-like leaves. The edible portion of the tree is the distinctive blue-black seed cones (commonly called 'berries') which appear in the autumn. They are too bitter to eat raw but are used to add flavour to a variety of dishes. Because of their diuretic properties, large quantities of juniper berries should not be consumed by pregnant women or young children.

*Cookery:* Juniper berries are very bitter and should not be eaten raw. They can, however, be used (sparingly) to flavour a number of dishes and in Europe have traditionally been used as part of meat and fish recipes as well as flavouring some alcoholic spirits (indeed, the original gin recipe used juniper berries; the word gin is derived from the French *genévrier*, meaning juniper).

Juniper berries are astringent and work best with strong-flavoured meats such as rabbit, hare, venison and game birds, or with fish such as salmon and turbot. In general, one should take four to six berries, crush them and then apply to the surface of the meat or fish with other seasoning, spices and marinades before roasting. Juniper berries may also be used to flavour vegetable dishes (see cabbage recipe below) or as an ingredient in meat pies. Try adding half a dozen berries to a meat paté recipe or to a game pie.

*JUNIPER CABBAGE*

Chop an onion and two garlic cloves and fry in butter or olive oil for 2 mins; add half a dozen juniper berries and cook for a further few minutes. Add about 500g of washed, shredded cabbage leaves (or a wild alternative, such as sea beet) and stir-fry over a medium heat for 10 mins, until soft. Season with salt and pepper and serve.

*Historical Uses:* Juniper berries and their derivatives (including 'juniper oil') have been afforded many curative properties, but they are believed to be especially beneficial for disorders of the kidneys, bladder and urinary tract such as cystitis, infections and prostate trouble. It has also been prescribed for chesty coughs, asthma and is said to have been used as a contraceptive jelly in historical times.

*Scientific Notes:* The juniper tree is one of the few plants in this book that is a conifer and thus related to the pine trees. It specifically belongs to the cupressaceae family and is a cousin to trees such as the giant sequoia. Juniper berry oil has measured antibacterial and antifungal properties, but tests using extracts as a mouthwash produced no effect on plaque or oral diseases. Juniper berry extracts have been tested for their ability to destroy certain cancerous cells but the results, while positive, have no medical application as yet. Tests on juniper extracts given to type 2 diabetic patients revealed only a small influence on their blood glucose levels.

## Rowan – *Sorbus aucuparia*

> 'It is a beautiful tree on the hills of the north, intermingled as it is with the dark pines and the waving birch.'
>
> Jeffreys Taylor, 1835

- Alternative Name: Mountain Ash
- Moderate-sized tree which grows wild across the British Isles (including mountain sites) but which is also cultivated in urban areas, parks and gardens.

The attractive rowan tree is a common sight, both in the countryside and about towns and villages. In the autumn the tree produces clusters of red berries that are a delight to the local bird population and passing foragers, although they should not be eaten raw. Rowan berries are outstandingly bitter and are mildly poisonous before cooking. They have been a food source for centuries, especially in northern parts of Britain and Europe where they offered a valuable source of food during the winter months.

*Cookery:* Rowan berries begin to ripen in late summer but it is traditional to wait until the mid to late autumn (preferably after the first frosts) before picking as this lessens the fruits' bitterness. As stated earlier, rowan berries should not be eaten raw.

The berries are generally used either as an ingredient in rowan wine (which requires about 2kg of fruit) or, more commonly, as an ingredient in a jelly. The astounding bitterness of the fruit and lack of pectin makes it preferable to combine them with another fruit, such as apples or blackberries. However, those who require a jelly for use as a condiment to roast meat may use rowan berries alone.

*ROWAN AND APPLE JELLY*
Take a good quantity of mixed apples and rowan berries (the ratio is not important) and place in a heavy pan with a little water. Bring to the boil and keep boiling and stirring until the mixture is soft and pulpy; this may take half an hour to an hour, depending on the quantity of fruit. Strain the pulp into a bowl using a muslin bag (this will take several hours). Measure the liquid obtained and place in a heavy pan; for every 500ml of liquid, add 450g of sugar and dissolve. Boil vigorously and remove any surface scum until the

mixture reaches the setting point (see Preparation Technique for details of this). Test by placing a blob on a fridge-cold plate and pushing a finger through it; if the mixture wrinkles up then it is ready. Pour into jam jars and seal immediately.

*Historical Uses:* The rowan tree is much mentioned in European folklore with its wood frequently being used to ward off ghosts, witches, spells and other supernatural malevolence. However, the fruit has been little mentioned in the usual herbalist sources although it has been prescribed to relive upset stomachs and piles.

*Scientific Notes:* The rowan tree is part of the rose family (Rosaceae). Neither the tree nor the berries seem to have been the subject of much attention by the pharmaceutical industry, although its extracts are alleged to be high in antioxidants and to have some antimicrobial properties.

## English Oak – *Quercus robur*

> 'The bark of this tree, possesses a large share of astringency, which it yields to water.'
>
> John Murray, 1808

- Etymology: Celtic, *quer*, beautiful; *cuez*, tree
- Large tree; common across the British Isles, including in parklands and towns.

The oak tree is so well-known that it probably needs little introduction. Despite its familiarity, the oak is not often thought of as a food source but the acorns, which are excessively bitter and are rich in tannin, can be turned into a substitute for coffee. Indeed, they were apparently used as such during World War Two, when real coffee was in short supply.

*Cookery:* Acorns ripen in the autumn and may be gathered from the tree or as windfalls. There are a number of different methods of preparing acorn coffee, but the one I prefer involves boiling the kernels which softens them and also removes some of the bitter tannin.

Add the acorns to a large pan along with plenty of water. Bring to a boil and continue boiling, uncovered, for 15 mins. Drain the acorns, let them cool and then peel them. Let the resultant kernels dry out completely; this may take several days and is best done in an airing cupboard or similar. Place in a coffee grinder and reduce to the same consistency as ground coffee. Place the granules on a baking tray in a warm oven and roast, giving them a shake until dark brown (but not burnt). Use the resultant acorn coffee (which may be kept in an airtight container) in the same way as you would use filter coffee (in a cafetière or with filter paper); begin by using about the half the quantity compared to normal coffee, then afterwards adjust the volume according to taste.

**Above:** *Rowan berries (p. 108).*

**Left:** *Oak tree (p. 109).*

**Below:** *Pignut (opposite).*

*Historical Uses:* Oak trees play a major part in British folklore and the bark was particularly prized by apothecaries because of its astringent qualities. Extracts of bark would be used in cases of dysentery, internal bleeding and severe pulmonary complaints as well as haemorrhoids and *prolapsus ani.* The acorns were said to be a diuretic and also to be helpful with inflammations, fevers and instances of poisoning.

*Scientific Notes:* Oak trees are part of the oak and beech family (Fagaceae). Many biological aspects of the oak have been subject to scientific inspection, but it would appear that this common and familiar tree has not been viewed with much interest by the medicinal and pharmaceutical communities.

## Pignut – *Conopodium majus*

> 'They provoke lust exceedingly, and stir up those sports she is mistress of.'
>
> Nicholas Culpeper, 1652

- Alternative Names: Earth Chestnuts, Ground Nuts, Cipper Nuts, St Anthony's Nut
- Perennial; woodlands and grasslands across the British Isles. Flowers white and arranged in umbels, leaves small and fern-like.

Pignut is a plant whose small tuber is frequently used by foragers to demonstrate their countryside skills. Once widely eaten, pignuts are currently the subject of legal restriction and may only be taken with the landowner's permission. Pignut tubers are fiddly to find and have an earthy taste that will not suit every palate, but there is a definite satisfaction to be gained in foraging for them. That said, the few times that I have foraged for them, I was guided by a friend who knew where to look and how to identify the plants. Given the potential hazards associated with this plant (see below), foragers who are beginners should perhaps consider looking for them with an experienced forager.

WARNING. There are several instances of people having eaten poisonous plants mistaken for the pignut, including the bluebell and the potentially fatal hemlock water dropwort, *Oenanthe crocata.* Make absolutely certain of your identification before consuming and, if in any doubt, do not eat.

*Cookery:* Pignut is an exceedingly tricky plant to locate and it is illegal to dig up and remove plants without the landowner's permission. They are at their best in the early spring and are common in bluebell woods, where the plant tucks itself among the patches of bluebells. The bulb of the bluebell plant looks similar to the tuber of the pignut but is poisonous: **make doubly extra sure that you have dug up a pignut bulb and not one belonging to a bluebell!** Otherwise the plant may be found in fields, meadows or open heath but make sure that you have the landowner's permission before removing any plants and beware of its similarity to some of the hemlock plants (see above).

It is the tuber (sometimes called a nut or a bulb) of the pignut that is edible, but this may be buried anywhere between 2 and 15cm below the ground. To retrieve this, hold the plant by the stalk and use a small trowel or knife to guide you downwards to the tuber. Once you are sure you have got a pignut tuber (and not some other bulb), simply scrape or rub away the brown skin and it is ready to eat.

Pignuts have a hot and nutty taste and may be eaten raw in the field but in my experience they are best chopped and eaten as part of a salad (allow about three pignuts per person). They may also be used as a garnish or as a general ingredient in soups.

*Historical Uses:* Traditionally believed to be an aphrodisiac, the other virtues afforded to pignut are its qualities as a diuretic and also as 'a remedy for the spitting and pissing of blood'.

*Scientific Notes:* Pignut is part of the carrot family (Apiaceae). The medical community's main concern with the pignut is with the number of people who have poisoned themselves by eating other plant species by mistake (see above).

## Sweet Woodruff – *Galium odoratum*

- Alternative Names: Wild Baby's Breath, Sweet-scented Bedstraw
- Etymology: Greek, *gala*, milk
- Perennial; shaded woodlands across lowland British Isles but rarer in northern Scotland. White flowers, leaves spear-shaped and radially arranged.

Sweet woodruff is a distinctive, sweetly-scented plant that seeks out damp, shaded places in woods and forests. The plant is used whole to add flavour to drinks but it is mildly toxic and can cause damage to the kidneys and liver if consumed in large quantities. For this reason woodruff may no longer be used as a food ingredient, although it is still used to flavour alcoholic drinks in some countries.

*Cookery:* Sweet woodruff may be foraged for during the late spring and summer. Cut the plant above the root, wash it then bruise the leaves, flowers and stem. It should be eaten sparingly and not at all by those taking blood-thinning products or with kidney and liver damage. To taste, place a few sprigs in a cup, add hot water then, after a few minutes, strain to make a scented, refreshing, green tea. Alternatively, add a few leaves to a vodka bottle and leave for a few days, or dry the leaves and flowers and use as part of a potpourri.

*Historical Uses:* The smell of sweet woodruff is retained by the dried plant and bunches of it were used to ward off insects, and especially moths, in linen cupboards and larders. The leaves were sometimes used to dress wounds and extracts of the plant were said to have sedative properties and to be useful as a restorative tonic for people recovering from illness. It was also said to be beneficial to the major organs, especially the liver (but see above!).

*Scientific Notes:* Sweet woodruff is part of the bedstraw family (Rubiaceae). It contains coumarin, a compound which provides its scent and has measured anticoagulant properties. It has been recommended that patients on blood-thinning products should not consume large quantities of sweet woodruff. Extracts of the plant are known to have antimicrobial effects.

## Common Hogweed – *Heracleum sphondylium*

> 'It is gathered in Sussex for the fattening of hogs, being known by the name of hogweed.'
>
> James Smith, 1814

- Alternative Name: Common Cow Parsnep (Parsnip)
- Etymology: named after Hercules who allegedly fed the plant to pigs
- Perennial; common in woodlands, roadsides and meadows across the British Isles. Small, white flowers arranged in tall clusters, leaves are rough and uneven.

Common hogweed has been praised for its asparagus-like culinary qualities but there are several cautions associated with foraging for and eating this plant. The most serious of these is its similarity to another species, the outsized giant hogweed (*H. mantegazzianum*), which is not only inedible but may actually cause harm to some people. The two species are reasonably easy to distinguish, not least because the giant hogweed may grow to a height of four metres. Be aware also of hemlock (*Conium maculatum*) which resembles hogweed but is highly poisonous (the leaves of hemlock are much more finely divided; see introductory section). Those whose skin is delicate or light-sensitive should consider wearing gloves when harvesting common hogweed as the plant's sap may lead to blistering. The young stems are the best part of the plant and may be gathered in the spring and early summer.

*Cookery:* Common hogweed should be harvested during the early spring when the plant is young. Choose smaller plants and take only the youngest, softest shoots as anything else will be too tough to eat. As stated above, make sure that you are picking common hogweed and not some other similar-looking plant such as hemlock (very poisonous) or giant hogweed (inedible and toxic). Do not eat the shoots raw.

To cook, strip the shoots of their bristly outer skin, wash them, then steam or boil for 10 mins or until tender. The shoot should now resemble asparagus both in appearance and taste, and may be served with butter as a starter or side dish. Cooked hogweed may also be used as a chopped ingredient in pasta or rice dishes, such as risotto.

*Historical Uses:* Common hogweed has been associated with a number of ailments but especially chest complaints such as asthma, congested lungs and coughs. Extracts of the plant have been used to relieve headaches, dizziness, jaundice and blocked ears.

Sweet woodruff (p. 112).

Broom flower (opposite).

Sweet woodruff (p. 112).

Broom bush (opposite).

Common hogweed (p. 113).

*Scientific Notes:* Hogweed is part of the carrot family (Apiaceae). The ability of hogweed to induce skin photosensitivity has been the subject of chemical investigation, but the plant has not been subject to any laboratory or clinical trials with regard to any potential pharmaceutical properties.

## Common Broom – *Cytisus scoparius*

> 'The plants form beautiful objects, considered separately, yet they often destroy the unity of expression of the scenery.'
>
> John Claudius, 1838

- Alternative Name: Scotch Broom
- Large bush; common on open ground and hedgerows across the British Isles. Large, yellow flowers arranged along the branches.

Broom is a distinctive and attractive bush which in late spring produces a proliferation of bright yellow flowers. Although an attractive addition to the British countryside, broom is considered to be a nuisance in some New World countries, where it has spread unchecked after being introduced. The culinary value of broom is limited and centres mostly on the flowers, which taste bitter and may be harvested during the spring.

*Cookery:* Although not currently popular in culinary terms, at one time broom had some uses, most of which focus on the bright yellow flowers which may be picked between April and June. For example, in pre-Victorian times it was said that the flower buds would be picked and used in recipes in place of capers. The buds are actually quite bitter and are certainly not an exact replacement for capers but they may be eaten raw or used in salads.

The other use for broom was in the brewing industry where it was one of a number of plants that was used to give beer an aromatic bitter flavour before the routine use of hops. The young branches were used when brewing beer, while with wine, handfuls of open flowers would be added prior to fermentation.

*Historical Uses:* The medicinal uses of broom are apparently few. Infusions made from the leaves have been used as a diuretic and preparations from the seeds and flowers are said to help cure gallstones and to induce vomiting. This latter quality is said to have led to broom being employed as an emetic cure for madness in eighteenth-century mental institutions.

*Scientific Notes:* Broom is a member of the pea family (Fabaceae). A laboratory testing using extracts of broom discovered that the plant appeared to offer hepatoprotective properties (i.e. it protects the liver against certain toxins).

## Wild Cherry – *Prunus avium*

- Alternative Name: Gean
- Etymology: Greek, *proune*, a plum
- Deciduous tree; native across much of the British Isles but also common in gardens and parks. White flowers in umbels.

Popular these days as an ornamental tree, the wild cherry is a native tree that has been used as a food source by humans for thousands of years. The cherry fruit ripens from midsummer onwards, moving from yellow to a dark red-black. There is sometimes a competition between foragers and birds as to who can get at the cherries first: it is a competition that the birds will often win. The cherries have a tart taste when ripe. Remember to get permission if the cherry tree is situated in a garden or park.

*Cookery:* The fruit from the wild cherry tree should be harvested when ripe, during midsummer to early autumn. The cherries have a variety of uses and may be used as a general cooked fruit in pies, jams, etc., especially when combined with blackberries, currants, apples and other sweet fruit. I present here a traditional recipe which requires a quantity of the fruit.

*WILD CHERRY JELLY*
Take 1.5kg of cherries and place in a heavy pan with 700ml of water and cover. Boil for about 20 mins or until the cherries are soft and mushy and the stones are freed from the flesh. Place in a muslin jelly bag and strain into a bowl (this will take several hours). Measure the resultant liquid and place into a heavy pan with 450g of sugar and the juice of one lemon for every 600ml of strained juice. Dissolve the sugar and then boil vigorously, stirring and removing any surface scum until the setting point is reached (see Preparation Technique for details of this). Ladle into clean jam jars and seal immediately. Unopened, it will keep for several months.

*Historical Uses:* During the eighteenth century water infused with extract of cherry stone was a popular remedy for adults and children, but in Victorian times the practice ceased when it was discovered that the potion was poisonous. The cherry fruit were not afforded much medicinal stock although they were said to be good for indigestion. Extracts from the tree, however, were frequently used to alleviate colds, increase appetite and improve eyesight.

*Scientific Notes:* The cherry tree is part of the rose family (Rosaceae). There does not seem to have been any testing on the medical properties of the wild cherry, although many of its agricultural properties, such as propagation, have been closely studied.

## Wild Raspberry – *Rubus idaeus*

> 'It growth not wild that I know of, except in a field by a village in Lancashire.'
> John Gerard, 1597

- Alternative Names: Framboise, Raspis, Hindeberry
- Etymology: Celtic, *reub*, to tear, because of its thorns
- Perennial; common in woods and hedgerows across the British Isles. White flowers on long thorny stems.

The wild raspberry is a close relation to the bramble and has the same scrambling, prickly stems which spread themselves laterally. The soft red raspberry is familiar as a supermarket fruit and has many of the same uses as the blackberry but is especially popular as a pudding ingredient. Wild raspberries are not as common as brambles, but with searching and a little local knowledge they may usually be found in a given area. The fruit ripens during summer, ahead of the blackberries, and may be gathered directly from the bush.

*Cookery:* Raspberries should be foraged direct from the plant in the late summer and autumn when the fruit is red and soft. They have a multitude of domestic uses and may be eaten raw or used as an ingredient in a variety of sweets and puddings. Any modern cookery book will provide quick and easy recipes involving raspberries, so I have provided three more unusual dishes from an 1826 domestic manual.

*RASPBERRY CAKES (1826 recipe)*
Pick out any bad raspberries that are among the fruit, weigh and boil what quantity you please, and when mashed, and the liquor is wasted, put to it sugar the weight of the fruit you first put into the pan. Mix it well off the fire until perfectly dissolved, then put it on China plates, and dry it in the sun. As soon as the top part dries, cut with the cover of a canister into small cakes, turn them on fresh plates, and when dry, put them in boxes with layers of paper.

*RASPBERRY BRANDY (1826 recipe)*
Pick fine dry fruit put into a stone jar and the jar into a kettle of water or on a hot hearth till the juice will run strain and to every pint (570ml) add half a pound (225g) of sugar give one boil and skim it when cold put equal quantities of juice and brandy shake well and bottle. Some people prefer it stronger of the brandy.

*RASPBERRY VINEGAR-WATER (1826 recipe)*
Put a pound (450g) of fine fruit into a china bowl and pour upon it a quart (1.1 litres) of the best white wine vinegar. Next day strain the liquor on a pound of fresh raspberries and the following day do the same but do not squeeze the fruit only drain the liquor

*Wild cherries (p. 116).*

*Wild raspberries (p. 117 and below).*

*Black currants (opposite).*

*Red currants (opposite).*

as dry as you can from it. Dilute with water according to taste. This is one of the most delightful drinks that can be made.

*Historical Uses:* Raspberries and blackberries were often lumped together by apothecaries and were afforded the same general medical properties. This includes their use as a general aid to those suffering from sore throats and colds and as a general health food for the undernourished.

*Scientific Notes:* Like brambles, the raspberry plant is part of the rose family (Rosaceae). Raspberries are noted for their high levels of antioxidant compounds which, according to one study, remain active for at least six months after the fruit has been processed into jam, etc. Wild raspberries also contain a chemical called ketone which, during laboratory trials, displayed possible anti-obesity properties in rats although this has yet to be proven to work on humans. Raspberry ketone has, however, been tested on human skin where (over a period of months) it apparently stimulated hair growth on the scalp and reduced skin elasticity on the face.

## Black and Red Currants – *Ribes nigrum* and *R. rubrum*

> 'The berries we could never obtain, except from gardens, as the birds feed on them before they are ripe.'
>
> James Smith, 1801

- Alternative Name: Quinsy Berry
- Etymology: An Arabian name for a gooseberry-like plant
- Medium-sized shrub; prefers damp or waterlogged ground, often in woodland or copses. Occurs across the British Isles. Green, bell-shaped, drooping flowers which are downy (black currant) or smooth (red currant).

Closely related to the gooseberry, black currants are probably most commonly consumed in the form of the sweet, syrupy cordials sold commercially and loved by children. The actual berries, which are usually available in supermarkets, are not as sweet as these cordials might suggest and have a sharp taste. They make for good eating, especially when combined with other summer and autumnal fruits. The fruit may be abundant and will ripen from early summer onwards.

*Cookery:* Both black and red currants ripen during the summer and are best harvested by picking entire bunches of fruit, stems and all. Top and tail the berries by putting the fruit and stems into the freezer overnight; then place the frozen fruit into a container and shake vigorously so that the stems and 'tops' fall away.

Red and black currants may be consumed raw and are delicious when eaten with cream or crème fraîche or as part of a fruit salad. They may also be combined with other fruit, such as raspberries, blackberries and apples, as part of a pie or summer pudding. In historical times it was common to turn the currants into either a cordial syrup or a jelly, the former being used as a drink while the latter would be served as a condiment with meat dishes. Currants are also widely used in wine-making and are an ingredient in some alcoholic drinks (e.g. cassis).

*TRADITIONAL BLACK CURRANT SYRUP*
The recipe requires a good quantity of fruit (a kilo or more) which should be weighed, bruised, cooked and then strained through a fine sieve to remove pips, stalks, etc. Then add just under double the weight of sugar to the original weight of the fruit. Simmer gently and bottle. Dilute with hot or cold water to make a delicious drink.

*CURRANT JAM AND JELLY (based on an 1822 recipe)*
Strip the fruit and stew them in a saucepan of water by boiling it on the hot hearth; strain off the liquor and to every pint (570ml) weigh a pound (450g) of loaf sugar; put the latter in large lumps and stir till nearly dissolved then boil in a preserving pan simmer and skim as necessary. When it will jelly on a plate put it in small jars or glasses.

*Historical Uses:* Naturally enough it is the berries that have mostly interested herbalists although extracts from the plants' roots was sometimes used to break virulent fevers. Currants were commonly administered as a syrup or in the form of a jelly, in which state it was considered to be a general health tonic and to be of especial use for colds, coughs and sore throats. The currants have also been cited as being beneficial in instances of indigestion, flatulence, measles, smallpox and infectious skin diseases.

*Scientific Notes:* Currants are part of the gooseberry family (Grossulariaceae). Currants are high in a variety of antioxidants and for this reason alone are often cited as being generally beneficial to a person's wellbeing, but recent tests on kurokarin, a compound extracted from black currants, suggest that the fruit may have antiviral properties as well. Laboratory tests suggest that kurokarin has an effect on certain types of influenza and herpes viruses; the pharmaceutical implications of this are being explored.

# *Chapter Four*

# Grasslands and Heath

Almost all the British grassland and heath habitats are man-made, having once been woodland areas that were cleared and then subject to livestock grazing. In fact, these open habitats are only maintained by the continual munching action of sheep, cows and goats, or by more systematic management such as tree clearance and controlled burning. Without this, the grasslands would soon be given over to shrubs, trees, brambles and fast-growing plants. Following years of neglect and loss to the plough, there has been a more concerted attempt to encourage and conserve grasslands and heaths, especially in the more crowded areas of southern England.

Many grasslands and heaths occur on hillsides with shallow chalky or acidic soils. This restricts trees but does favour shrubby bushes and a number of fragrant, aromatic plants which may be loosely called 'herbs'. Bushes, such as gorse and bilberry, will be pretty obvious while other plants may be found hidden away among taller grasses or in and around shrubs.

The delicate nature of grassland and heath environments (plus their beauty and leisure potential) has led to some popular sites being designated as nature reserves or Sites of Special Scientific Interest. Often these designations will affect only a small area. For example, the grassy chalk down near to my former home in Hertfordshire was home to a rare species of flower, but the conservation measures applied only to the small area in which it grew. As ever, check a map and look out for signs indicating nature reserves, private property, etc. Other than this, show general consideration for the environment and your health and safety by following the general guidelines given in the introductory section. Be careful when searching undergrowth and make sure of your identification so that you don't accidentally pick a rare species. Watch out for snakes during the spring and summer months!

*A mature grassland is a beautiful and important environment.*

## Bilberry – *Vaccinium myrtillus*

> 'The bilberry is at once agreeable, delicate, rich, nutritious, and easy of digestion.'
>
> Anon, 1843

- Alternative Names: blaeberry, whortleberry, whinberry (or winberry), wimberry, myrtle blueberry, fraughan, black-hearts
- Etymology: Latin, *vacciniae*, berries, because of its fruit
- Wild fruit bush; found in acidic soil on heaths and open woodland across much of Britain (a related species, the bog bilberry, may be found in marshy areas in the north). Green-pink flowers, leaves are serrated with an erect, angled stem.

***Above and right:*** *Bilberries.*

The bilberry is closely related to the North American blueberry and the much rarer European cranberry (not to be confused with the American cranberry). The bush produces a profusion of blue-black berries which may be harvested in the late summer and autumn. They taste similar to blueberries and may be eaten fresh from the tree or used in a variety of culinary dishes.

*Cookery:* Bilberries were a very popular historical food and I have seen several passages in Victorian books which praise their delights. The berries were traditionally eaten raw with cream, sugar or even milk, while the young leaves have sometimes been used as an ingredient in mixed fruit teas. It is still possible to buy bilberry jam in some British (and almost all French) supermarkets.

In the modern kitchen the bilberry has many potential uses but they are especially popular in dessert dishes, such as fruit puddings and fruit salads, or as an ingredient for jams, jellies and in wine-making. To make bilberry jam or jelly, simply follow the recipe given for red currants (*q.v.*); below is an adapted Victorian recipe for bilberry gin.

*BILBERRY GIN/VODKA*

Take a half-empty bottle of gin or vodka, add two tablespoons of sugar and shake well until dissolved. Fill to the neck with washed bilberries and invert the bottle several times. Leave for three months, inverting the bottle every couple of days or so. Towards the end of this time taste and add a little more sugar if desired. When satisfied with the flavour, strain the berries and re-bottle the resultant spirits. Do not discard the alcohol-soaked fruit; boil it with other autumn fruit and eat with cream or crème fraîche.

*Historical Uses:* Confusion between the bilberry, cranberry and bog bilberry makes it difficult to discern the medicinal properties afforded specifically to the bilberry, but it seems that the fruit were used raw or as a syrup to aid digestion and promote general good health. It is suggested by some herbalists that bilberries may be helpful to those suffering from diabetes and arthritis.

*Scientific Notes:* The bilberry plant is part of the heather family (Erinaceae). Extracts from bilberries have been demonstrated to inhibit the growth of certain types of leukaemia cells during laboratory trials, although the fruit themselves are not being suggested as a cure for this disease. Compounds within bilberry leaves have shown a positive effect on the blood disorder dyslipidemia (again in laboratory trials). The belief that bilberries might enhance night vision has been proven false by several clinical trials, although other studies using just the extracted compound anthocyanoside have had more positive results with regard to arthritis.

## Wild Chamomile – *Anthemis nobilis*

> 'The scent betrays it if trodden upon. This quality has induced some curious people to plant chamomile for a green walk in gardens.'
>
> James Smith, 1810

- Alternative Names: Roman Camomile, Chamomile, garden camomile, ground apple, low chamomile, English chamomile, whig plant
- Etymology: Greek, *anthos*, a flower
- Perennial; on grasslands and gardens in the southern British Isles. White, daisy-like flower; leaves are feathery and finely divided.

The chamomile plant is found on dry heaths, grasslands, roadsides and gardens across the southern British Isles but it tends to be somewhat localised in its occurrence. There are several similar species one of which, the stinking chamomile, is aptly named and does not possess the pleasantly aromatic scent that characterises this wild flower. The chamomile flowers appear in the early summer and have been praised for their scent, which resembles apples or quinces (the plant's common name means 'ground apple'), since Egyptian times. In rare cases some people have developed allergic dermatitis from contact with chamomile or its products.

*Cookery:* Wild chamomile flowers, which are daisy-like, should be picked during the late spring and summer; try avoiding older, well-established plants as their flavour can be a little sharp in comparison to the aromatic, soothing taste of younger specimens.

In the kitchen chamomile has few uses other than as the ingredient for a soothing hot beverage. This is easily made by placing a large handful of flowers (fresh or dried) into a teapot and then adding boiling water. After several minutes, pour the tea into cups using a strainer, adding sugar or honey if desired. In historical times herbalists would recommend consuming a pint or more of chamomile tea a day in order to stave off digestive troubles and nightmares.

*Historical Uses:* Apothecaries had many uses for chamomile flowers, which would be picked, dried in bunches and then infused in water (sometimes oil would be extracted from the flowers but this requires a prohibitive quantity). In such a form chamomile would be used to break fevers, relieve indigestion, aid sleep, remove headaches and promote relaxation. Chamomile tea remains a popular drink and there are recent controversial claims by Japanese scientists that this drink may help in cases of diabetes or kidney disease.

*Scientific Notes:* The wild chamomile is one of several closely related species within the broader daisy family (Asteraceae). Extracts from chamomile have been tested as mouthwash with negative results other than one Middle Eastern study which recommended chamomile mouthwash for patients undergoing radiotherapy. Other than this, there appears to have been very little interest in chamomile as a medicinal or pharmaceutical plant.

## Red Clover – *Trifolium pratense*

> 'When young, the flower-head has the appearance of extreme woolliness or pubescence.'
>
> George Sinclair, 1826

- Alternative Names: wild clover, cleaver grass, marl grass, cow grass, trefoil, purple clover
- Etymology: Latin, *tres*, three; *folia*, leafed
- Perennial; common on grasslands across the British Isles. Red flowers on an erect stem; leaves spear-shaped.

Red clover was once widely used by farmers as a plant whose nitrogen-fixing ability would revive tired soil. It would usually be sown in the spring with barley, oats, wheat or rye. The advent of artificial fertilisers has made red clover a rare sight on agricultural land these days, but it may still be extremely common on grasslands and other open places across the British Isles, where it will tolerate a variety of soil types.

*Cookery:* The plant's pinkish-red flowers have a sweet, aromatic taste and should be picked between the late spring and early autumn. The culinary uses of red clover are rather limited but the flowers can be used raw in salads and to give flavour to home-brewed wines and beers; however, it is not a major constituent in food dishes. To make your own red clover tea, add a tablespoon of flowers (raw or dried) to boiling water; leave to infuse for a few minutes then strain. Add sugar or honey if needed.

*Historical Uses:* Apothecaries used red clover flowers to treat skin complaints such as eczema and for various complaints associated with the menopause. Some modern herbalists also recommend red clover for menopausal women (see below), the advice sometimes being to drink tea from the flowers or to suck on the raw buds.

*Scientific Notes:* Red clover is part of the pea family (Fabaceae). The plant possesses weak oestrogenic properties, but clinical trials to determine whether it may be useful in the treatment of menopausal symptoms have had negative results. Caution has been expressed at the presence of coumarin in red clover as this substance may interfere with certain blood-thinning drugs.

*Wild chamomile (p. 124).*

*Red clover (p. 125).*

## Corn Salad – *Valerianella locusta*

- Alternative Names: Lewiston Corn Salad, Lamb's Lettuce, Field Salad, Rapunzel
- Etymology: Latin, *valeo*, powerful, based on its presumed health-giving properties
- Annual; grasslands, sand dunes and some urban areas. Pinkish flowers in clusters on spikes; leaves fleshy, lettuce-like.

Corn salad is a common plant which colonises a variety of dry places such as farmland, grasslands and even old walls. It is sometimes thought of as a weed but the plant is not tenacious and was said by one Victorian agriculturalist to be a 'humble intruder on tillage lands'. This is also the 'rapunzel' plant that, in the fairy tale of that name, grew in the garden of the wicked witch. By Victorian times corn salad was no longer an important domestic food, but most domestic manuals would list it as being a useful plant to add to salads.

*Cookery:* Corn salad leaves possess a pleasing flavour that is milder and less bitter than that of many wild salad plants. It is the young leaves that are of most use and these should be gathered during the spring, before the plants bolt, and again in the autumn. (One historical source says that the leaves are at their best when they have a 'brownish cast'.) The plant is often associated with lighter, sandy soils so wash it especially well to remove any coarse particles. Its principal use is, as the name suggests, as a raw ingredient in salads but it may also be used as a garnish or to flavour light vegetable soups.

*Historical Uses:* In medieval times it was cultivated in smallholdings where its leaves were a popular source of food. It was also widely used by herbalists who preferred the root to the leaves; extracts would be applied to those suffering from intestinal parasites and spasmodic fits. It was also popular as an aromatic additive to baths and perfumes.

*Scientific Notes:* Corn salad is part of the valerian family (Valerianaceae) and is one of several closely-related species. The plant has not been deemed worthy of examination for any potential medical or pharmaceutical properties, although some aspects of its cell biochemistry have attracted the attention of horticultural scientists.

**Above and right:** *Corn salad.*

## Common Gorse – *Ulex europaeus*

> 'And what more noble than the vernal furze,
> With golden baskets hung ? Approach it not,
> For every blossom has a troop of swords
> Drawn to defend it.'
>
> James Hurdis, 1788

- Alternative Name: Common furze
- Etymology: Celtic, *uile*, all; *ec*, prickle
- Evergreen shrub; found across the British Isles in open, wild places such as hillsides, headlands and heaths, especially those which have thin, acidic soil. Numerous small yellow flowers on very thorny branches.

For all its prickly thorns, the gorse bush was once a popular plant with farmers; it would be cultivated for a variety of reasons including for hedging and as shelter for cattle. It was also widely grown because the branches made an excellent fuel for ovens (see below) and could be used as cattle food as well. Gorse is geographically widespread about the British Isles and is often locally common. In recent years, the invasive nature of gorse, and its ability to cause 'gorse fires', has led to it being declared a menace in some environmentally sensitive regions such as heaths and headlands.

*Cookery:* In some parts of Britain, such as Cornwall, gorse was burnt in ovens to help flavour baked food such as pies. The popularity of this practice led to the saying that 'the Devil will not come to Cornwall for fear of being put into a pie'. Aside from its use as an oven fuel, the principal domestic use of gorse is as an additive to the wine and beer-brewing process. It is the distinctive yellow flowers that are used and these may appear at any time but usually occur in profusion during the spring; this is also the best time for picking them as the flavour is stronger.

Gorse tea is a favourite drink but it requires a surprising number of flowers (one to two handfuls), so should be in made either in a jug or teapot. Tip on boiling water and leave for several minutes before straining. Another family favourite is gorse cordial which is made in much the same way as elderflower cordial (*q.v.*).

*GORSE CORDIAL*
Put three or four handfuls of gorse flowers in a bowl and cover them in about 500ml of boiling water. Stir in 220g of sugar and the rind and juice of a lemon. Leave to infuse for several hours, stirring occasionally. Strain through a fine sieve and place in a clean, capped bottle for storage. When required, dilute the cordial with water, adjusting the taste with sugar or honey if necessary.

*Historical Uses:* Traditional medicine practitioners did not much favour the plant although the flowers, when infused in hot water and drunk, were said to cleanse the body and especially the kidneys.

*Scientific Notes:* Gorse is a member of the pea family (Fabaceae). The principal scientific interest in gorse revolves around a chemical compound in the plant which can be used to mark certain types of cancer cells (this does not mean that the plant has any proven anti-cancerous properties).

## Heather – *Calluna vulgaris*

> 'Gem of the heath! Whose modest blooms shed beauty o'er the lonely moor.'
> Mrs Grant (nineteenth-century poem)

- Alternative Name: Ling
- Etymology: Greek, *kalluno*, to clean, from its use as a broom
- Shrub; on heaths and moors across the British Isles. Flowers pink, small and bell-shaped; leaves small and in four rows along stem.

Heather is a classic heath plant and is particularly synonymous with Highland moors and lonely headlands. In such environments heather may be the most abundant plant, although it may also be found in a variety of other open areas and is especially associated with acidic soils. There are several related species but the most common are heather and bell heather (*Erica cinerea*), both of which have similar properties.

*Cookery:* Heather is not the best-tasting of plants, it being rather earthy and bitter. The flowers, which appear in the summer and early autumn, may be infused in hot water to produce an astringent-tasting tea. The culinary uses for heather are very limited with the only commonly repeated recipe being for 'heather ale', which I must confess to never having made but I reproduce an abbreviated Victorian recipe below. The origin of the ale is traditionally ascribed to the Picts and it is sometimes said that the Scots wiped out this ancient tribe because they would not pass on the brewing method.

*HEATHER ALE (1823 recipe)*
The ale of heather is made by brewing one part malt and two parts of the young tops of heather; sometimes hops are added.

*Historical Uses:* In the past heather has been used for a variety of purposes including as a fuel, thatching material, bedding, cattle fodder and for making brooms, but it is not generally held to have many medicinal properties.

*Common gorse (p. 128).*

*Heather (p. 129).*

*Scientific Notes:* Heather is part of the heather family of plants (Ericaceae). The ability of heather to survive in heavily polluted soils has interested some scientists, while others have expressed concern at the levels of mould and fungal toxins that have been measured in herbal teas made from the plant. The presence in heather of a chemical called quercetin is of interest as this compound is being investigated for a whole host of potential medical properties including its use to combat some cancers, heart disease and asthma. However, results thus far are inconclusive and there is even some evidence that large quantities of quercetin may cause the body serious harm.

## Salad Burnet – *Sanguisorba minor*

> 'The leaves taste and smell like cucumber, and give that flavour to salads, for which purpose this plant is very generally cultivated.'
>
> James Smith, 1813

- Etymology: Latin, *sanguis*, blood; *sorbes*, to absorb, from its use as a bandage
- Perennial; on grasslands and downs across the central and southern British Isles. Flowers form compact green heads; when bruised, the leaves smell of cucumber.

*Salad burnet.*

As its name implies, salad burnet was at one time cultivated in gardens for use as a domestic food. It is, however, a wild plant that is most common along the chalk grasslands of England and Wales. It has a cucumber-like taste and even smells of cucumber when the leaves are lightly crushed between the fingers.

*Cookery:* In culinary terms, young salad burnet leaves should be picked in springtime and used raw in salads. In historical times, bunches of salad burnet would be gathered and placed inside casks of wine and beer, where it was said to improve the flavour and/or correct imperfections that may have arisen during fermentation. The salad option remains the best modern use for this plant but the bruised leaves also make a pleasant addition to summer drinks such as home-made lemonade, Pimms and quaffable white wines.

*Historical Uses:* Salad burnet was popular with herbalists both for its leaves, which smell of cucumber when crushed, and the root which is bitter and acrid. Various infusions or extractions from these would be used for stomach complaints or in cases of asthma, scrofula and toothache. It was also popular as a skin improver with the leaves being said to be able to remove freckles.

*Scientific Notes:* Salad burnet is part of the rose family (Rosaceae). Clinical trials suggest that salad burnet may help prevent the development of stomach ulcers. Extracts from the plant have also been shown to have anti-HIV properties when tested on laboratory cell cultures, although the wider pharmaceutical potential of this has yet to be explored.

## Sow Thistle – *Sonchus oleraceus; S. asper*

> 'Much sought after by hares and rabbits; and gathered for tame ones.'
>
> Samuel Gray, 1821

- Alternative Names: Hare's Colwort, Hare's Thistle, Milky Tassel, Swinies
- Etymology: from the Greek for hollow
- Annual; widespread in many environments across the British Isles but thrives best in disturbed, grassy locations. Yellow, dandelion-like flowers; leaves broad, pointed and either matt with few spines (smooth sow thistle) or glossy with many spines (prickly sow thistle).

There are several species of sow thistle in Britain but the commonest are the smooth (*S. oleraceus*) and the prickly (*S. asper*) ones. At the end of the eighteenth century the sow thistle was described as being 'a troublesome weed' that was fit only for feeding rabbits and sheep. However, only a few decades previously the sow thistle formed a part of the countryside subsistence diet. It remains a common plant that is often associated with hedgerows and agricultural ground but which may also turn up in a variety of grassy places right across the British Isles. Be wary of foraging for plants growing by busy roads as there is a suggestion that the sow thistle may adsorb car-derived pollution.

*Cookery:* Traditional culinary uses for the smooth sow thistle include the use of its leaves as a salad ingredient or boiled as a green side-vegetable. The leaves have a similar taste to lettuce and should be picked in the spring and summer when young. Wash them well and add to mixed green salads. The leaves of the prickly sow thistle are less palatable but its roots were at one time dried and ground into flour for use in baking bread.

*Historical Uses:* Since ancient times herbalists have found a variety of uses for the sow thistle. The milk from the stalks is said to have helped asthmatics and those suffering from kidney and bladder stones, while the leaves and stalks were said to help breast-feeding women produce 'well-coloured' children. The leaves were prescribed to soothe skin complaints, itching and haemorrhoids, while compounds containing sow thistles would be placed in the ears to relieve deafness and tinnitus.

*Scientific Notes:* The common sow thistle is one of several closely related species in the daisy family (Asteraceae). Aside from being high in anti-oxidant compounds, laboratory trials suggest that the sow thistle may possess significant anti-anxiety properties which are probably related to the presence of hydroethanolic and dichloromethane in the plant's leaves.

## Yarrow – *Achillea millefolium*

> 'This plant has an agreeable weak aromatic smell, and a bitterish, rough, and somewhat pungent taste.'
>
> William Woodville, 1810

- Alternative Names: Common Yarrow, Gordaldo, Nosebleed plant, Old Man's Pepper, Sanguinary, Milfoil, Soldier's Woundwort, Thousand-leaf, Thousand-seal
- Etymology: after Achilles, who allegedly used it as a bandage
- Perennial; widespread in grasslands, meadows and verges across all the British Isles. Pinkish flowers; leaves woolly and leafy.

Yarrow is a common plant in meadows and rough areas across the British Isles. It was once a popular cattle food and would be encouraged to grow in pastures but nowadays the plant is either ignored or considered to be a weed. The plant has a bitter, astringent taste and its use in the kitchen was infrequent, but the plant would occasionally be foraged for food.

*Cookery:* Yarrow has a bitter, astringent taste and there are few historical references to the plant being regularly used as a food source. Where it is mentioned, it is invariably the

Sow thistle (p. 132).

Wild marjoram (opposite).

Yarrow (p. 133 and opposite).

young leaves, which appear in the spring and summer, which get boiled up and served as greens. Yarrow is said to have been used as a salad ingredient but the bitter taste will probably not suit modern palates. The plant is best exploited by placing some shredded leaves into boiling water and allowing it to infuse into a tea. The addition of honey greatly improves the flavour.

*Historical Uses:* Apothecaries had several uses for yarrow and would prescribe it externally for use on ulcers, infected wounds (Achilles is said to have used it for this purpose in ancient Greece) and for baldness. Taken internally it was said to be helpful for dysentery, menstrual problems and toothache.

*Scientific Notes:* Yarrow is a member of the daisy family (Asteraceae). Its flowers have been tested for their anti-inflammatory properties, with some success, while essential oil derived from the plant has known antioxidant and antimicrobial effects. Extracts from the plants have been shown to repel certain species of malarial mosquito, while at least one laboratory study credits yarrow with the prevention of gastric ulcers.

## Wild Marjoram – *Origanum vulgare*

> 'There is scarce a better remedy growing for such as are troubled with a sour humour in the stomach.'
>
> Nicholas Culpeper, 1652

- Alternative Names: Oregano, Grove Marjoram
- Etymology: Greek, meaning 'joy of the hills'
- Perennial; locally common in grasslands in the southern British Isles. Purple flowers; egg-shaped, downy leaves.

Wild marjoram is not a native species but is said to have been introduced into the British Isles from southern Europe in the sixteenth century. The plant has a distinctive aromatic, herb-like smell and a pungent taste that somewhat resembles thyme. It is an important herb in many forms of cookery. The leaves should be picked from spring until autumn and may be dried for use over winter.

*Cookery:* For centuries wild marjoram has been used as an herb to flavour stews, broths and light cakes and that remains its greatest culinary use to this day. The leaves should be picked, washed and chopped before use. Treat the leaves like an aromatic herb and add to a variety of traditional modern dishes in the same quantity and manner as other similar plants such as thyme and basil. It is especially good with meat and vegetable stews, but will work as a minor ingredient in soups, salads and pasta dishes. In early autumn consider picking leaves (or even whole plants, if growing in a non-sensitive area) and drying them for use over winter.

*Historical Uses:* The medicinal properties afforded to wild marjoram are similar to those that have been ascribed to thyme and these cover an extraordinary list of ailments including: indigestion, headaches, baldness, tuberculosis, leprosy, deafness, liver disease, and as an antidote to certain poisons. The leaves would often be used raw or the oil extracted from them for later use, as drying was thought to lessen the plant's potency. A common headache powder of the seventeenth century was formed from an equal combination of dried sage, betony and wild marjoram.

*Scientific Notes:* Wild marjoram is part of the dead nettle family (Lamiaceae). Essential oil of wild marjoram has notable antifungal properties that may have some commercial applications in inhibiting the growth of yeast and other fungal organisms. Laboratory tests have found wild marjoram to have some beneficial effects on diabetic rats by acting as an anti-hyperglycaemic compound.

## Wild Thyme – *Thymus polytrichus*

> 'The plant is aromatic, though sometimes very slightly so.'
>
> James Sowerby, 1803

- Alternative Names: Mother of Thyme, Creeping Thyme
- Etymology: Greek, *thumos*, strength, because of its scent
- Perennial; found on dry heaths and grasslands across the British Isles. Purple flowers, ascending stem, ovate leaves; smells faintly of thyme.

Wild thyme has many of the same properties as the better known domestic herb found on sale in supermarkets, but its flavour and aroma are usually not so strong and may sometimes be almost totally lacking. The wild plant has an aromatic smell and generally the stronger the scent it emits, the more flavoursome the leaves will be. Also, and although sprigs of wild thyme may be picked at any time of year, the flavour of wild thyme is generally at its strongest in the summer when the plant is in flower.

*Cookery:* Wild thyme should be used as an herb and as such it is often used to add an aromatic flavour to a wide variety of dishes. A look through Maria Rundell's 1826 *New System of Domestic Cookery* reveals over thirty recipes which required a sprig or pinch of thyme; these range from poached fish to soups, omelettes and meat dishes as well as a large range of sauces.

Sprigs of wild thyme may be used whole in dishes (but remember to take them out before serving) or the leaves and flowers can be stripped from the plant, washed and added whole or chopped. Sprigs and leaves of wild thyme may be dried in an airing cupboard or similar for later use. Always remember that you will need to add more of it than the cultivated thyme found in supermarkets and herb gardens. Wild thyme also makes a good herbal infusion; simply place a good sized sprig into boiling water and leave for several minutes.

*Historical Uses:* Wild thyme has been afforded many uses including, according to Nicholas Culpeper, 'the spitting and pissing of blood, coughing and vomiting'. It is also said to be useful in cases of indigestion, stomach cramps, hyperactivity and lethargy. Often it was not necessary to eat the herb but merely to anoint the afflicted part of the body with a concentrated extract of the plant.

*Scientific Notes:* Wild thyme is part of the dead nettle family (Lamiaceae). The ability of wild thyme to thrive in soils polluted by heavy metals has interested some scientists, but the plant itself has not been assessed for any health-giving or pharmaceutical properties.

## Wild Basil – *Clinopodium vulgare*

- Alternative Names: Woodland Basil, Cushion Calamint
- Etymology: Greek, *clino*, bed; *podium*, small foot
- Perennial; only locally common on dry grasslands in southern England. Purple flowers in bristly clusters on the leaves; smells of basil.

The wild basil plant is readily identifiable in the wild by its distinctive aromatic smell. It has a long historical pedigree as a culinary herb that has been used to flavour a great range of dishes for millennia. However, its flavour is generally less strong than the domestic variety (this is true of many wild herbs), and so you will require a greater quantity of leaves than would be the case with basil obtained from a supermarket.

*Cookery:* The leaves of the wild basil can be picked during the spring and summer and may be dried for later use. This is an herb plant which can be used generously to add a delicious aromatic flavour to salads, pasta and rice dishes as well as soups, broths and fish dishes. This herb works particularly well with olive oil-based dressings and vegetable risottos.

*Historical Uses:* In the seventeenth century Nicholas Culpeper remarked that his fellow herbalists were in violent disagreement ('like lawyers') about the medicinal properties of basil. Some believed it to be poisonous, while others held it to be a great cure for headaches, fevers and various stomach complaints. Culpeper himself recommended it for use on wasp and hornet stings, snake bites and other venomous creatures. He associated the plant with the breeding of these animals and recounted the story of a man who smelled the herb and afterwards 'had a scorpion breed in his brain'. Wild basil is widely used in Eastern Europe for binding ulcers and wounds.

*Scientific Notes:* Wild basil is part of the dead nettle family (Lamiaceae). The plant has been shown to have strong antibacterial qualities leading to suggestions that it might have a pharmaceutical use. Extracts from the plant have a known effect on some cancerous tumours in the laboratory but the real world applications of this are uncertain.

Wild thyme (p. 136).

Wild basil (p. 137).

## Cowberry – *Vaccinium vitis-idaea*

'The berries are red, acid and unpleasant until baked.'
Samuel Gray, 1821

- Alternative Names: lingonberry, foxberry, mountain cranberry, red whortleberry, lowbush cranberry, red bilberry
- Etymology: Latin, *vacciniae*, berries, because of its fruit
- Evergreen shrub; on thin acidic soils in highland regions of northern England, Northern Ireland and Scotland. Flowers pink and bell-shaped; leaves evergreen and dotted beneath.

The cowberry is a low straggling shrub that prefers moist, acidic soils associated with open woodlands and moorland. It is a sub-Arctic plant that is generally restricted to upland regions in the northern British Isles. It is the small, red berries that are edible and these are generally harvested in the autumn months. It is revered in Scandinavia and parts of Germany, but remains largely unheard of here other than in Scotland and select areas of northern England.

*Cowberries.*

*Cookery:* The berries possess a bitter, acidic taste and are not very palatable when eaten raw. In historical times the berries would be rendered edible with the addition of sugar or molasses; as such cowberries would be incorporated into puddings, fruit pies and, most often, made into a jelly which would be used as a meat condiment. In Sweden cowberry jelly remains a popular food which is eaten with a variety of foods, from sausages to pancakes, and in recent years it has been popularised in America, where it is sold in supermarkets as 'lingonberry jam'.

*COWBERRY JAM/JELLY*
Place 1kg of washed cowberries in a heavy pan with 250ml of water and boil, stirring occasionally, for 10–20 mins until soft and pulpy. Add approximately 500g of sugar and dissolve. Boil vigorously for several minutes until setting point is reached (see Preparation Technique for details of this). Pour into clean jam jars and seal at once.

If making jelly then place the cowberry pulp in a muslin bag and strain into a bowl; this may take several hours. Measure the resultant liquid and place in a heavy pan. For every 600ml of liquid add 500g of sugar and dissolve; boil vigorously for several minutes until the setting point is reached.

*COWBERRY PUDDING (1838 recipe; untested by the author)*
A pint (570ml) of milk, with a little salt and a little molasses, stirred quite stiff with flour, and a quart (1.1 litres) of berries stirred in gradually with a spoon, makes a good-sized pudding. Leave room for it to swell and let it boil three hours.

*Historical Uses:* Herbalists used cowberries to relieve the effects of colds and flu and especially sore throats. In mainland Europe cowberries were used to treat some venereal diseases, including gonorrhoea, as well as digestive complaints such as diarrhoea.

*Scientific Notes:* The cowberry bush is part of the heather family (Ericaceae). Aside from acknowledging a high level of antioxidant chemicals and tannins, there has been little scientific research into the biological effects of cowberries.

## Crowberry – *Empetrum nigrum*

> 'Chiefly the food of mountain birds or quadrupeds, though sometimes eaten by mankind.'
>
> James Smith, 1821

- Etymology: Greek, *en*, in; *petros*, stone, because of where it grows
- Evergreen shrub; on thin acidic soils in highland regions of northern England, Northern Ireland and Scotland. Pink flowers; leaves small with margins meeting at the back.

The crowberry (not to be confused with the similar-sounding cowberry) is only found in highland parts of Britain and is only common in Scotland. The berries are tart and time-consuming to gather in quantity, but nonetheless were once important in some sub-Arctic cultures, especially in northern Sweden, Finland and Iceland. There the berries would be gathered in the autumn and winter for use in wine-making or as a supplement in a hunter-gatherer lifestyle.

*Cookery:* I have not personally foraged for crowberries and the information in this section comes from a friend of mine. I am assured by him that crowberries are very tart and are best used as the ingredient for a jam or jelly. The recipe given for cowberries should be followed (*q.v.*) and, if short of fruit, it is possible to add cowberries or bilberries to the mixture.

*Historical Uses:* Scandinavian tradition holds that crowberries may help relieve stomach complaints, eye infections and kidney stones, but other applications have included its use in cases of epilepsy, nervous disorders and even anthrax.

*Scientific Notes:* The crowberry plant is part of the crowberry family of plants (Empetraceae). Crowberries are rich in antioxidants and some laboratory studies have linked the plant with general health-giving properties. In common with some other wild berries, crowberries have noticeable levels of quercetin, a compound which is being extensively investigated for its potential medical qualities (see entry for heather).

## Common Poppy – *Papaver rhoeas*

- Alternative Names: Corn Poppy, Field Poppy, Flanders Poppy, Red Poppy, Wild Rose, Cup Rose, Cheese Bowls
- Etymology: Celtic, *pap*, a milky juice
- Annual; widespread across grasslands, pasture and disturbed areas. Rarer in the north than the south. Flower is large, red and papery.

The poppy is an iconic plant which was known in historical times as the 'corn rose' for its ability to grow among cereal crops. Such a habitat is typical of this species, which likes disturbed ground, and explains why it was one of the first plants to colonise the churned-up battlefields of World War One. There are four species of poppy with red flowers in Britain; three of these are more common in the south and east of England with just one, the long-headed poppy (*P. dubium*) being more widespread further north.

*Cookery:* The culinary uses for poppies in Britain are limited and centre on the seeds. These may be found inside the plant's distinctive seed-heads which appear in the late summer and are ready for foraging during the early autumn. In both historical times and modern times the seeds have been used as decoration on loaves of bread, cakes and

**Above and below:** *Crowberry (p. 140).*

*Common poppy flowers and seed-heads (p. 141).*

*Poppy seed-head (p. 141).*

biscuits. However, poppy seeds are often added to cake mixtures and to sweet desserts, such as rice pudding, to add a nutty, aromatic flavour. This practice is more common in northern and eastern Europe than in the British Isles but there are some native poppy seed recipes.

*POPPY SEED CAKE*

Take 225ml of milk and place into a saucepan with 110g of poppy seeds. Heat gently until simmering, then cook for half an hour. In a bowl cream 225g of butter with 225g of sugar; add three egg yolks, whisk and then fold in 225g of flour and two teaspoons of baking powder. When thoroughly mixed, add in the poppy seed and milk mixture. Whisk three egg whites until stiff, then fold into the mixture. Place the mixture in a medium cake tin and cook in an oven for 45–60 mins at 180°C. Rest cake for a few minutes before removing from tin and allowing to cool on a wire tray. For the frosting, beat 50g butter until smooth, then add 75g of full-fat cream cheese and half a teaspoon of vanilla essence. Slowly stir in 100g icing sugar and then spread over the cake.

*Historical Uses:* Poppies were well-known in ancient cultures and there was much admiration for their beauty and, in the case of the opium poppy, for their medical properties. The common poppy does not produce opium but some historical herbalists nonetheless produced syrups and drinks from its seeds which were said to aid sleep and relieve the symptoms of tuberculosis. Others probably recognised the difference and declared that the common poppy was only useful in cases of fainting and gluttony-induced vomiting.

*Scientific Notes:* The common poppy is a member of the poppy family (Papaveraceae). There has been little investigation into the medical properties of the common poppy, it perhaps being overshadowed by its more famous opium-producing cousin.

## Mint – *Mentha* spp.

> 'It is a remedy for those that have venereal dreams and pollutions in the night, being outwardly applied to the testicles or privates.'
>
> Nicholas Culpeper, 1652

- Etymology: Greek, *mintha*, old name for the plant
- Perennial plants that are generally found growing on damp soil in association with grasslands and meadows. Some may be found close to waterlogged ground. Distribution and abundance varies but most species are widespread with the plants being rare only in northern Scotland.

There are several species of mint in the British Isles, both in the wild as well as in gardens, where it is grown as an herb. The most frequently eaten species are:

Water Mint (*Mentha aquatica*); found in or near water.
Corn Mint (*Mentha arvensis*); widespread and common.
Spearmint (*Mentha spicata*); widespread and common.

All these species offer the distinctive mint smell and flavour that we are familiar with, and although there is a subtle difference between the species, the leaves may be picked and used in the same manner.

In addition to the above three common species, there are two other types of mint which are generally rare and should not be picked. These are: round-leaved mint (*Mentha suaveolens*) and pennyroyal (*Mentha pulegium*).

*Cookery:* Mint is essentially an herb and as such it is the leaves that should be gathered, preferably before the plant flowers in the summer. The leaves do not hold their flavour when dried and so should be used immediately or placed in vinegar or oil. There are several uses for mint and one may in general follow the recipes that are given in modern cookery books, directly substituting wild leaves for the quantities of mint given. For a refreshing summer drink, try placing several cucumber slices with several wild mint leaves in a large jug of iced water.

*Historical Uses:* Mint has had a variety of medicinal uses, some aspects of which still survive to this day. Mint was, for example, much used to solve digestive problems, especially upset stomachs and indigestion (still reflected in mint-flavoured antacid tablets). The list of other uses is extremely long and ranges from helping women with 'swollen, sagging or great breasts' to those with halitosis, scrofula, parasites or even suspected cases of rabies. There are few ailments which have not at some time had mint prescribed for them.

*Scientific Notes:* The various species of British mint are all in the dead nettle family (Lamiaceae). Mint plants contain menthol, a compound that is famous for its ability to induce a cool, refreshing feeling when inhaled or applied to the skin. This occurs because menthol triggers the body's cold receptor cells, inducing a feeling of coolness. There have been many minor medical applications for menthol, including in some cough and cold remedies, but it is also widely used as a flavouring in foods, cigarettes and drinks.

## Catmint – *Nepeta cataria*

> 'If you set it, the cats will eat it. If you sow it, the cats will not know it.'
>
> Anon

- Alternative Name: catnip
- Etymology: Greek, *neap*, a scorpion, whose sting it was said to cure
- Perennial; on grassland and downs mostly in southern England. Flowers are white; leaves are heart-shaped.

**Above:** *Corn mint (p. 144).*

**Below:** *Spearmint (p. 144).*

*Water mint (p. 144).*

*Catmint (p. 145 and opposite).*

*Wild parsnip (opposite).*

I have included catmint not so much as a human delicacy, but because of its popularity with our domestic felines. In 1837 Benjamin Barton wrote of this plant: 'Cats are extremely fond of it, especially when it is withered, when they will roll themselves on it, tear it in pieces, and chew it as long as a leaf remains.' Many commercial products for cats are impregnated with catmint (usually under the name of catnip) but the leaves and stems of the wild plant are just as effective. It should be noted that catmint is believed to be in decline in the wild, so please take particular care when foraging for this plant.

*Cookery:* I can find no instances of catmint being willingly eaten by humans as its taste is very bitter. Cats, however, love it and will often go wild in its presence. Gather the leaves and stems in the spring and summer and either dry them for later use or bruise them in the presence of a cat and watch its reaction!

*Historical Uses:* Catmint has been administered in cases of chesty coughs, bladder disorders and jaundice. It is commonly presented in the form of a drink, the leaves having been boiled or distilled to extract their juice.

*Scientific Notes:* Catmint is a member of the dead nettle family (Lamiaceae). The plant contains nepetalactone, an active ingredient which is known to act as a repellent against certain annoying insects, including mosquitoes. Research is ongoing to develop an effective natural insect repellent from catmint.

## Wild Parsnip – *Pastinaca sativa*

> 'It nourisheth much, and is good and wholesome, but a little windy.'
>
> Nicholas Culpeper, 1652

- Etymology: Latin, *pastus*, food
- Perennial; not uncommon in chalk grasslands and sandy soil in southern Britain. Yellow flowers; leaves are ovate and downy beneath.

The wild parsnip is locally common in southern England and was used as a food plant for centuries until the larger domesticated varieties of parsnip arrived during the Middle Ages. Wild parsnips have many of the same taste qualities as the farmed varieties but there are a couple of warnings associated with foraging for it. The first is that the plant can be confused with **the highly poisonous hemlock** (*Conium maculatum*) so check your identification carefully. The second is that the plant's sap may cause skin irritation (including blistering and photosensitivity), so consider wearing gardening gloves and long sleeves. As might be expected, it is the root of the plant that is edible and this is best harvested in the early winter (see Introduction regarding the uprooting of wild plants).

*Cookery:* Wild (and domestic) parsnips benefit greatly from the early winter frosts and so it is best to harvest this plant late in the year, around November or December time. It is the smaller roots (those about the size of a carrot) that hold the best flavour, but their size can be a nuisance as it may take a while to gather a sufficient quantity and then a further while to clean and prepare them for cooking.

The wild parsnip holds many of the same properties as the domesticated variety and may be used for food in the same manner. They may be steamed (my preference), boiled, roasted and added to casseroles, soups, etc., in the same manner as farmed parsnips. Note Nicholas Culpeper's warning about parsnips and flatulence – there may be some truth in it.

*Historical Uses:* Wild parsnip seeds were long deemed to be an aphrodisiac, while the root was viewed as an excellent general health food, especially for those suffering from undernourishment or recovering from serious illness. The plant's caustic sap was thought to act as an antidote to snake and insect bites (see warning above).

*Scientific Notes:* The wild parsnip is part of the carrot family (Apiaceae). The roots contain a measurable amount of furanocoumarin compounds, some of which are known to interfere with the action of conventional pharmaceutical drugs (although there are no specific warnings against consuming parsnips in this regard). There are also instances of dermatitis arising from contact with the parsnip plant.

# *Chapter Five*

# Wetlands and Streams

Of all Britain's complex natural ecosystems, it is the wetlands, streams and rivers that have probably suffered the most damage and destruction during recent years. Marshes and bogs have been drained, streams dammed, flood plains built upon and tonne upon tonne of pollution tipped into various lakes and rivers, sometimes rendering them almost uninhabitable by all but the hardiest of organisms. Matters have improved, especially concerning water quality, but even as I write there is a stretch of the River Trent that has been badly contaminated by an industrial leak of cyanide. All this is a tragedy, not just from an ecological viewpoint, but because many wetland areas can serve a useful function by absorbing the floodwater that annually threatens towns, villages and cities across Britain.

The term wetland covers a broad range of environments and may include everything from small mountain bogs to square kilometres of fenland. Many wetland plants are specialised and endemic, a situation which renders them nationally threatened, even if they are locally common. Therefore in this chapter I have included only a handful of the more widespread and easily recognisable edible species. These could well be growing close to rare plants, so be careful where you are putting your feet. Also think of your own safety when near rivers, lakes and canals and do not take risks in search of plants. It is surprisingly difficult for a fully-dressed person to haul themselves out of the water, especially if it is cold or the river/lake has steep sides.

It is irritating to have to relate (yet again) the threat of human-inspired pollution but this may be an especial problem within wetland environments. There are, of course, risks from industrial-derived discharge and sewage, but in Britain this tends just to affect rivers and is less of a hazard now than it was a few years ago. As far as the forager is concerned, it is pollutants from farming that probably present the greatest hazard. Streams that pass through agricultural land may receive input from slurry, farm machinery or the faeces of cows, sheep and other livestock. This could affect even the clearest-looking mountain stream which may, for example, have passed through rough grazing pasture. In some areas there is also an issue with farm chemicals (particularly fertilisers, herbicides and pesticides) entering the groundwater, where they may lurk for some years before emerging in springs. Also, the anoxic (i.e. lack of oxygen) conditions present in some marshy areas and slow moving streams will cause the precipitation of heavy metals, especially in organic-rich sediments. Fortunately most of this pollution can be washed

*Britain's wetlands are delicate, so tread carefully.*

*Bog myrtle (opposite).*

off the plants in the kitchen, but it does mean that you should avoid eating unwashed raw plants from wetland areas.

A salient reason for not eating raw aquatic plants is the presence of liver flukes such as *Fasciola hepatica* which enters the water from animal waste and which may cause fascioliasis, an unpleasant and sometimes dangerous disease. The most common means of human liver fluke infection in Europe is via eating contaminated plants such as watercress, so do not be tempted to nibble on a few leaves while you are out of doors. Any plant that has partially or wholly grown in a stream, pond or lake should be taken home, washed and cooked thoroughly before eating. It is a shame to have to offer such advice, but it is better to be safe than sorry.

## Bog Myrtle – *Myrica gale*

> 'The berries exhale a delightful fragrance when rubbed between the fingers.'
>
> James Smith, 1803

- Alternative Names: Sweet Gale, Goule, Gaule, Sweet Willow, Wild Myrtle, Dutch Myrtle
- Etymology: Latin, *Myrica*, a tamarisk
- Shrub; typical of boggy ground in most parts of the British Isles. Leaves spatulate and toothed.

Prior to the drainage of low-lying marshes and fenlands, shrubs such as bog myrtle were a much more common sight about Britain but even so, it remains widespread and may be locally common. The plant has had a variety of historical uses including the catkins which, according to pioneering botanist Carl Linnaeus, would be boiled and the resultant scum skimmed off and formed into candles. The leaves are aromatic with a distinctly bitter taste and may be gathered in the summer.

*Cookery:* The culinary uses of bog myrtle are limited by its astringent taste. In medieval times the leaves were used in the brewing industry to impart a bitter taste to beer. This practice all but ceased with the discovery of hops, although it is alleged that peasants in some parts of Europe were brewing with bog myrtle by preference until a few decades ago. Bog myrtle leaves have also been used as an herb when cooking meat and to add flavour to wine. Those wishing to use this herb in the kitchen should include a handful of leaves in their home-brewed wort to add flavour but I would not recommend using this plant as a direct substitute for hops.

*Historical Uses:* The leaves of bog myrtle were deemed to have few medicinal properties but were said to drive away moths, fleas and ticks. It was not uncommon for the leaves to be stuffed into wardrobes, clothes and mattresses as an insect repellent, a practice which still continues to the present day.

*Scientific Notes:* This plant is a member of the bog myrtle family (Myriceae). Chemical extracts from bog myrtle have been shown to be effective at repelling ticks and other undesirable arthropods, including some species of mosquito. The plant is high in antioxidants but it has not been tested for its pharmaceutical properties, although one study did mention bog myrtle as a species which should be investigated for medicinally beneficial compounds.

## Lady's Smock – *Cardamine pratensis*

When daisies pied and violets blue,
And lady-smocks, all silver-white,
And cuckoo-buds of yellow hue
Do paint the meadows with delight.

Shakespeare, *Love's Labour's Lost*

- Alternative Name: Cuckoo Flower
- Etymology: Greek *kardia*, the heart, and *damao*, to fortify, from its medicinal properties
- Perennial; damp areas and water meadows across the British Isles. Flowers pale lilac, in clusters on tall spikes.

Folklore once held that the beautiful, delicate flowers of lady's smock belonged solely to the fairies and that picking them would bring bad luck. This superstition was not just beneficial to the lady's smock but also to the orange-tip butterfly (*Anthocharis cardamines*) which feeds upon the flowers. Its two common names are said to be derived from the flowers tending to appear around the time of Lady Day (25th March) which is also when the first cuckoos can be heard. The plant is found across the British Isles where it inhabits damp, grassy places such as water meadows and stream banks but it may also occur in gardens, if conditions are suitable.

*Cookery:* Young lady's smock leaves have a fresh, peppery flavour similar to that of watercress and were at one time readily gathered in the springtime for use in salads or as a garnish to soups. The plant is delicate and beautiful but it is becoming scarce in some parts of Europe and, although not endangered, it is inadvisable to gather large quantities of leaves. Take just enough to add to a salad or as a substitute for cress or watercress in sandwiches.

*Historical Uses:* Lady's smock was once considered to be on a par with watercress, to which it is related, the flowers being 'excellent good for the scurvy; they provoke urine, and break the stone, and excellently warm a cold and weak stomach, restoring lost appetite, and help digestion'. Other suggested properties include an alleged ability to help epilepsy while, in northern parts of Britain, the whole plant would be picked and pounded to extract the juice for use as an antidote to indigestion and kidney stones.

*Scientific Notes:* Lady's smock is part of the cabbage family (Brassicaceae). It has not been investigated for any medicinal properties it may hold.

## Meadowsweet – *Filipendula ulmaria*

- Alternative Names: Queen of the Meadow, Pride of the Meadow, Meadow-Wort, Meadow Queen, Lady of the Meadow, Dollof, Mead Sweet and Bridewort
- Perennial; in wet pastures and damp ground all around the British Isles.

Once known as 'queen of the meadow', this is a common, fragrant plant of damp regions such as marshes, meadows and stream banks. In the late spring and summer it produces a beautiful spray of small, delicate white flowers which have a distinctive sweet smell. Archaeologists have found evidence of meadowsweet inside Bronze Age graves, while in medieval times it was widely picked to add flavour to mead.

*Cookery:* The leaves and flowers of meadowsweet are quite bitter and were not eaten raw. They would be picked in spring and summer to flavour wine or for use in brewing beer. It also makes a pleasant herbal infusion which in times past would be taken as a cure for headaches. According to the herbalist Gerard, the leaves may be added sparingly to meat stews, while the flowers would be used ornamentally about the house. The root was said to be dried and ground into flour in Russia, and to have been used in the tanning industry.

*Historical Uses:* The leaves, flowers and roots were all used by herbalists in connection with such disorders as indigestion, dysentery and depression. The plant is also a traditional cure for headaches and fevers which is understandable as the plant contains salicylic acid, a constituent of the drug aspirin (which is itself named after *Spiraea*, the old name for meadowsweet).

*Scientific Notes:* Meadowsweet is a member of the rose family (Rosaceae). One laboratory study found some evidence that compounds within meadowsweet may have a suppressing effect on the body's immune system, although this has yet to be investigated fully. The plant is notable for its content of antioxidants and tannins, and is listed as a species which may be of interest to those looking for new sources of anti-cancer drugs.

## Watercress – *Rorippa nasturtium-aquaticum*

- Etymology: Saxon, *rorippen*, old name for this plant
- Perennial; in streams and brooks across the British Isles. Flowers small and white clustered in small spikes; leaves broad, fleshy and dark green.

Watercress is a familiar plant that inhabits shallow streams and brooks across most of lowland Britain. It has been known to the human palate for millennia and remains a popular food source to this day. Watercress is famed for the clean, peppery taste it can add to salads, sandwiches and soups. Sir Francis Bacon was especially fond of this plant

*Lady's smock (p. 152).*

*Meadowsweet (p. 153).*

*Meadowsweet flowers.*

*Watercress (pp. 153, 155, 156).*

and believed it to be 'friendly to life'. Watercress has been commercially cultivated in flooded beds since at least the early nineteenth century.

*Cookery:* The edible qualities of watercress will be familiar to many, it being a succulent, crunchy plant with a fiery taste. It can be gathered all year round for use in salads or as an ingredient or garnish for sandwiches. In such a form it may be eaten raw, the stalks and leaves being washed then ripped apart by hand. However, eating raw watercress is not currently advised as the plant may be home to the destructive liver parasite *Fasciola hepatica* which abounds in still and slow-moving waters. Instead, it is recommended that all wild watercress should be thoroughly blanched or cooked before it is eaten. It is particularly good in soup.

*WATERCRESS SOUP*

Take a large bunch of watercress and chop it finely. Melt a little butter or oil in a heavy saucepan and fry the cress with a splash of lemon juice. Cook for 10 mins. Beat an egg with a teaspoon of flour. Add it to the cress, then pour in three pints of vegetable stock. Boil for 10–15 mins, then serve as is or liquidise. For a thicker soup add potatoes or other root vegetables with the stock and then cook until they are tender, adding further water if necessary. Liquidise and serve.

*WATERCRESS SOUP (1836 recipe)*
Take twelve large red carrots, scrape them clean and put them into a stewpan with a quart (1.1 litres) of water; add cleaned turnips, celery, leeks, and onions, cut in pieces, and half a pint (285ml) of split peas. Stew all together till tender, adding some broth to prevent burning; then [stain or liquidise it], and put to the pulp five pints (2.8 litres) of [stock], and some blanched water-cresses; boil for twenty minutes, skim, season with salt, and serve. It should be of the consistence of pea soup.

*Historical Uses:* Herbalists considered watercress to be a powerful cleanser of the blood and a cure for scurvy (not surprising: it is high in vitamin C) and kidney stones. The leaves, when bruised and placed on the skin, were said to improve the skin, while immersing one's head in a basin of vinegar and watercress would act as a stimulant against drowsiness.

*Scientific Notes:* Watercress is a member of the cabbage family (Brassicaceae). It has not been widely studied for its medical properties, although it has a noticeable level of carotenoid compounds, the consumption of which has been generally linked to a healthy lifestyle.

## Common Comfrey – *Symphytum officinale*

> 'It is commonly gathered to supply the markets for medicinal use.'
>
> Philip Miller, 1835

- Etymology: Greek, *sumphuo*, to unite, for its healing properties
- Perennial; all British isles but rare in Scotland and Ireland.

Comfrey is a tall, attractive plant that favours damp and waterlogged soils such as are often associated with marshes, streams and ditches. It produces bell-shaped flowers that may be white, pink or purple in colour. A naturalised hybrid called Russian comfrey (*Symphytum x uplandicum*), may be found in some parts of the country, but this differs little from the common species in appearance or taste.

It should be noted that the United States Food and Drug Administration has recently issued a warning about the internal use of comfrey following the discovery of a probable link between excessive consumption of the plant and the development of liver problems, including tumours (see scientific notes below).

*Cookery:* Historically young leaves of comfrey would be picked in the spring, boiled and then served directly as a vegetable side dish. The flowers were sometimes also picked in the late spring and used to flavour cheap beer and wine. In modern cookery it is the young leaves that should be picked, washed and de-stalked; they may then be boiled or steamed and served with a little butter as a side vegetable. Alternatively, use the leaves as an herb to flavour dishes such omelettes, pasta dishes, pancakes or risottos.

*Historical Uses:* Herbalists used comfrey as a means of curing internal injuries such as ulcers, broken bones and bruising to internal organs, as well as finding it beneficial to flesh wounds and infections. It would also be given as an expectorant in cases of cold and influenza, and was said to ease the symptoms of gout and arthritis. Most parts of the plant could be used by herbalists but it was the roots that were most in demand: these would usually be prepared into a syrup or drink as this 1788 recipe for a domestic health tonic demonstrates:

*BOILED COMFREY ROOTS (1788 recipe)*
Take a pound (450g) of comfrey roots, scrape them clean, cut them into little pieces, and put them into three pints (1.7 litres) of water, let them boil till there is about a pint (570ml); then strain it, and when it is cold put it in a sauce-pan; if there is any fettling at the bottom throw it away; mix it with sugar to your palate, half a pint (285ml) of wine, and the juice of a lemon; let it boil, then pour it into a clean earthen-pot, and set it by for use. Some boil it in milk; and it is very good where it will agree, and is reckoned a very great strengthener.

*Scientific Notes:* Comfrey is part of the borage family (Boraginaceae). Laboratory trials involving excessive consumption of comfrey suggest that the plant may provoke serious liver disorders including the development of cancerous tumours. This is thought to be linked to the presence of hepatotoxic pyrrolizidine alkaloids within the plant which, while being removed in many commercial preparations of comfrey, are present in the wild plant. The seriousness of this research has led some people to class comfrey as a poisonous plant.

## European Cranberry – *Vaccinium oxycoccus*

- Etymology: Latin, *vacciniae*, berries, because of its fruit
- Evergreen; locally restricted to upland bogs. Rose-coloured and fuchsia-like flowers; leaves green with a threadlike stem.

The European cranberry should not be confused with the larger and more commercially familiar American cranberry. The European species is a denizen of upland peat bogs where it forms low shrubs that creep across the landscape.

*Cookery:* The edible part of the plant is the berries, which form in the late summer and autumn, turning to a bright red colour. They have an acidic taste which prevents them from being enjoyed raw, but they have in the past been combined with bilberries and other autumn fruits to produce jams and jellies. See the recipes for the bilberry and cowberry for further information.

European cranberry (p. 157).

Common comfrey (p. 156).

*Historical Uses:* Apothecaries afforded many of the same properties to cranberries as were attributed to crowberries, to which they are closely related. In this respect they have been used to relieve stomach complaints and kidney stones. However, in more recent years the cranberry has been widely promoted as a cure for the urinary disorder cystitis, in which respect it has many advocates (but see below).

*Scientific Notes:* The European cranberry is part of the crowberry family (Ericaceae). The berries contain notable quantities of anthocyanin compounds, some of which are being actively investigated for potential pharmaceutical benefits which include combating some cancers and neurological diseases. The ability of cranberries to relieve the symptoms of urinary tract infections (such as cystitis) has engendered a mixed reaction among scientists, with several studies finding evidence in favour of this while others are less positive. It has been suggested that the presence of proanthocyanidins in cranberries might prevent bacteria from being able to adhere to the bladder wall, thus preventing infections from taking hold.

# Chapter Six

# The Coastal Fringe

I was fortunate enough to grow up near the coast and it is the seashore which inspired my early interest in British natural history. Even now, rarely a day passes when I do not walk along the beach, even if only for a few minutes and sometimes I will spend hours there, searching among rocks and weed for shells, worms, starfish and other organisms. Of all the natural environments described in this book, it is the seashore where I feel most at home and it is where my first unwitting steps in foraging occurred when, as a teenager, I would pick and cook sea beet leaves, much to the alarm of my dear mother.

I have split the seashore into two chapters. This one will cover such edible plants as are to be found at or just above the high water mark or in the coastal ecosystems (such as sand dunes and marshes) that exist immediately landward of the shore. The next chapter

*A rugged coastline may be home to many edible plants.*

will focus on the seashore itself and the range of seaweeds (i.e. marine algae) which may be cooked and eaten.

The coastal fringe covers a variety of environments including cliffs, sand dunes, shingle banks, salt marshes and estuaries as well as man-made structures such as harbours, car parks and marinas. Many of these areas have been developed to encourage walkers and other tourists and will be readily accessible via footpaths, green lanes or other rights-of-way.

Coastal ecosystems such as marshes, dunes and estuaries may have been designated areas of scientific interest or of natural importance, in which case there will be severe restrictions on the picking of plants. Check a map to see which areas may be under restriction and look out for warning signs. If you are caught removing plants from a restricted area the penalties may be severe and ignorance is not considered an excuse. Even in non-restricted areas, minimise the impact of your presence by only taking what you need and showing regard for other plants and animals in the area. Be especially aware of the Wildlife and Countryside Act, which forbids the uprooting of plants on public land. When I have foraged for root plants such as wild carrot and fennel, I have done so with the permission of a landowner; I have also successfully grown these in my own garden. Even in well-managed areas there will be hazards, such as rising tides, crumbling cliffs and Ministry of Defence training areas. Use an OS Map to plan your route and check the weather forecast and tide table before heading out.

## Alexanders – *Smyrnium olusatrum*

> 'Aromatic, but too strong and pungent to be agreeable.'
>
> James Mackay, 1836

- Etymology: Greek, *smurnia*, myrrh, from its fragrant juice
- Biennial; mostly restricted to coastal regions of southern England and Ireland. Yellow flowers in tall umbels; leaves radial.

Alexanders is a locally common plant that is found on seaside verges, on cliffs or as a coloniser of overgrown plots and fields. It is traditionally held to be common on plots where monasteries once stood, the plant having at one time been cultivated by monks. Even outside monasteries, alexanders was once widely grown in gardens as a salad herb. Despite its popularity in late medieval times, many later authors speak of the plant's edible qualities with some disgust and its culinary position was usurped by celery whose popularity as a domestic vegetable was established during the nineteenth century.

*Cookery:* In historical times the fleshy stalks of alexanders would be picked, boiled and eaten with butter as a side vegetable or main dish. Sometimes the young leaves would also be picked and added to salads or placed in soups.

Alexanders is best foraged for during the springtime when the leaves and stalks are tender, although historically it was often gathered in the autumn. Only the first few inches of the leaf stalk above the ground are soft enough to be edible; therefore cut the stalks by cutting as close to the ground as possible and then discarding the top part. The stalks should be washed, then blanched in boiling water for several minutes (until tender) before being served either as a starter, with melted butter and black pepper, or as a side dish with fish or white meat.

The leaves were often added to salads and, in one 1812 cookbook, alexanders was listed as being the best salad plant ahead of cucumbers and artichokes. There are references to its leaves being added to stews, broths and soups.

*Historical Uses:* Herbalists used the roots and leaves to aid with disorders of the bladder and urinary tract, it being said to help with infections and to aid the passing of water. Juice from alexanders would be given in cases of indigestion and excessive flatulence.

*Scientific Notes:* Alexanders is a member of the carrot family (Apiaceae). The plant contains small quantities of a chemical called furanodiene which is being investigated for potential anti-cancer properties, especially in relation to cervical cancer. However, alexanders itself is not cited as a cancer prophylactic.

## Black Mustard – *Brassica nigra*

- Etymology: Celtic, *bresic*, a pottage made from this plant
- Annual; on sea cliffs, coastal verges and riverbanks across the southern British Isles. Yellow flowers; leaves stalked and bristly.

Cultivated for centuries for its ascribed medicinal properties, black mustard may be locally common in coastal regions of England and Wales, where it colonises fallow ground, roadside verges and cliffs. It forms tall, distinctive plants which produce a mass of yellow flowers in late spring and summer. The leaves may be eaten in the spring, while the much prized seed pods appear in late summer and autumn.

*Cookery:* Black mustard was at one time a common constituent of the kitchen garden, the young leaves being picked in spring for use in salads or to be blanched as greens. (The same is true of its close cousin rape, *Brassica napus*, whose young leaves are similarly edible.) It was, however, the seeds that were most highly prized and these would be extracted from the picked pods (a somewhat tedious job) in the late summer and autumn.

Black mustard seeds have a distinctive nutty flavour which may be released by lightly frying them in hot oil until they start to pop about the pan. This flavour lends them to being used in Asian cookery, where one can fry a handful of seeds before adding other spices and ingredients to form such dishes as curries and stir-fries. The seeds may also

Alexanders (p. 160).

Fennel (opposite).

Black mustard (p. 161).

be used sparingly to form salad dressings or as a garnish to pickled vegetables or other dishes with a significant quantity of vinegar.

*Historical Uses:* Apothecaries favoured using the oil that could be extracted from the seeds, either by compression or distillation, and then dissolved in alcohol or water. In this form black mustard would be administered as a purgative, antiseptic, defence against gut parasites and skin conditions such as itching. 'The only drawback is a strong penetrating and disagreeable smell,' wrote one Victorian apothecary.

*Scientific Notes:* Black mustard is part of the cabbage family (Brassicaceae). The seeds have been noted to contain relatively high levels of melatonin, a hormone which helps regulate daily biological rhythms in many animals, including humans. Melatonin has been linked to cancer prevention and in some countries (e.g. the USA) is available as a dietary supplement to help regulate people's wake/sleep patterns. (It should be noted that black mustard is not specifically cited as having anti-cancer properties or for being useful for regulating sleep.)

## Fennel – *Foeniculum vulgare*

'Every garden affordeth this plentifully.'
Nicholas Culpeper, 1652

- Etymology: Latin, *Foeniculum*, old name for this plant
- Perennial; mostly coastal in southern England and Wales. Yellow flowers in umbels; feathery leaves; aromatic smell.

For centuries the fennel plant was an essential part of the kitchen and medicinal garden, where it would be carefully nurtured. These days it is rarely seen in domestic gardens but the plant may be found growing wild in grassy verges and waste ground, especially close to the sea where it may sometimes occur in abundance.

*Cookery:* Fennel has many culinary uses and, although less popular these days, it is possible to buy the bulbs from most supermarkets. It has a pungent, distinctive smell and a familiar aniseed-like taste. The whole plant is edible; the leaves, flowers and stalks should be picked in the late spring and summer; and the seeds and bulb in the mid-autumn (see introductory section regarding the uprooting of wild plants). The bulb is root-like and not as bulbous or fleshy as the varieties of fennel that are sold in greengrocers and supermarkets. Fennel stalks may be picked and dried for later use and the bulbs stored for some weeks before use.

Most historical cookbooks list fennel as the perfect accompaniment to oily fish, especially mackerel, although it works well with most fish species, including salmon. The fish should be gutted and stuffed with fennel, then grilled (or cooked over an open fire or

BBQ) but this also works well when poaching. It is possible to use all parts of the plant with the fish, but the leaves and stems are probably the most convenient.

Other common uses for fennel include its use in salads and as a refreshing summer herbal infusion called the 'cooling waters of fennel'. The latter was made by placing fennel leaves in hot sugary water which is then left to cool down. Below are two historical recipes for fennel dishes involving fish.

*FENNEL SAUCE FOR FISH (1837 recipe)*
Wash and boil green fennel, mint, and parsley, a little of each, till tender; drain and press them, chop them fine, and add melted butter; serve up immediately. If the herbs mix long with the butter, they will be discoloured.

*FILLET OF MACKEREL WITH FENNEL AND GOOSEBERRIES (1759 recipe)*
Boil the mackerel, only adding a little vinegar and a bunch of herbs. Take the sides or fillets from the bone, and cut in two pieces; about four is enough for such a dish as here proposed, put them into a stew-pan, dash in a glass of white wine, some minced fennel, green onion and parsley, pepper, salt and nutmeg; stew all about eight or ten minutes. Put in about half a pint (285ml) of scalded young gooseberries whole; squeeze in a lemon or orange, and serve it up hot.

*Historical Uses:* The main prescription of fennel was (and still is) for digestive trouble including indigestion, flatulence and instances of food poisoning. Other uses include an alleged ability to cleanse the blood, liver and spleen, clear kidney stones and to stimulate the production of breast milk; it has also been used in cases of cold and influenza to help break a fever and, when dissolved in wine, is said to cure hiccups.

*Scientific Notes:* Fennel is part of the carrot family (Apiaceae). The plant is high in antioxidant compounds and is notable for its antimicrobial properties. Various aspects of the plant have been investigated in the laboratory with it being suggested that the plant may offer some protection to the liver and might be effective as a general anti-inflammatory and painkiller. The plant continues to be closely investigated in a variety of laboratory and clinical trials.

## Common Mallow – *Malva sylvestris*

- Alternative Names: Tall Mallow, High Mallow
- Etymology: Greek, *malache*, soft, from its leaves
- Perennial; all Britain but coastal and more common in south. Large purple flowers on long stems.

Various species of mallow have been eaten since at least Biblical times with the plant being cultivated by the Romans and ancient Greeks. Common mallow may be found on fallow ground and grass verges across much of Britain but it is more common in the south and central parts of England, Wales and Ireland. It is just the leaves that are picked and eaten with the best time for picking them being in the early spring, before the plant produces distinctive pink-purple flowers. The taste is a little like okra.

*Cookery:* The sixteenth-century herbalist John Gerard commented that mallow did not have a place in any respectable kitchen garden. Even so, the leaves were at one time widely eaten, usually as greens, and especially in coastal communities.

In springtime pick the youngest leaves, then wash them before boiling/steaming for several minutes. Serve as a side dish with butter. Mallow leaves on their own can be quite a heavy dish for modern stomachs, but smaller amounts of blanched leaves can act as a substitute for spinach in pasta and rice dishes or as an ingredient within a general soup.

*Historical Uses:* Apothecaries would use all parts of the mallow plant, including the flowers, roots and seeds, which would frequently be dissolved in milk. The plant was said to be generally beneficial to health, with the Roman Pliny commenting that whoever took a spoonful of mallow 'shall that day be free from all diseases that may come upon him'. More specific cures are said to include stomach ache, sore throats, lung diseases, dysentery, fainting, baldness and cases of poisoning.

*Scientific Notes:* Mallow is a member of the mallow family of plants (Malvaceae). A laboratory study suggests that mallow may have the ability to lower blood cholesterol levels, possibly because it contains elevated levels of compounds called anthocyanins. Other species of mallow may have anti-inflammatory properties.

## Marsh Samphire – *Salicornia europaea*

- Alternative Names: Glasswort, Saltwort, Jointed Glasswort
- Etymology: Latin, *sal*, salt; *cornus*, a horn
- Annual; Coastal; all British Isles except the far north. Fleshy green plant with jointed stem.

Marsh samphire is a distinctive, fleshy plant which has been much lauded by foragers for its crisp, salty asparagus-like taste. The plant grows very close to the sea on the muddy parts of salt marsh fringes or estuaries where it may tolerate periodic inundation by the tide. Prior to the mid-nineteenth century marsh samphire was valued for its high soda content and was commercially gathered (by 'samphire gatherers') for use in the glass-making industry.

Marsh samphire was also widely eaten both cooked and raw, with harvesting of the long fleshy stalks taking place along the seashore during the late spring and summer months, after the equinox spring tides had subsided (May is traditionally held to be the best month for gathering).

Common mallow (p. 164).

Marsh samphire (p. 165).

**Above:** Red valerian (opposite).

**Below:** Red valerian, white variety (opposite).

*Cookery:* Marsh samphire was a very popular food source and although it may be eaten raw when picked young, it is most commonly prepared by placing tied-up bundles of the plant into boiling water for ten minutes. This renders the leaves tender but the stalk remains woody, so it is best consumed by holding the plant by its root then using your teeth to scrape the loose flesh away.

Marsh samphire must be washed thoroughly to dislodge any detritus brought in by the tide. It does not keep for any length of time and is best eaten within a day of picking. Historically this problem was overcome by pickling the marsh samphire, for which a 1792 recipe is given below. In times past both boiled and pickled marsh samphire would be served up with roast meats.

*PICKLED SAMPHIRE (1792 recipe)*
Lay green samphire in a pan, and throw two handfuls of salt over it; cover with spring water, and let it lie twenty-four hours, then put it into a saucepan, throw in a handful of salt, and cover with good vinegar. Cover close, and set it over a low fire. Take it off the moment it is green and crisp, for, should it remain till soft, it will be spoiled. Put it in the pickling pot, and cover it close.

*Historical Uses:* Apparently once widely used by herbalists, marsh samphire fell out of favour during Tudor times and, by the seventeenth century, it was only being prescribed for digestive complaints and general wellbeing.

*Scientific Notes:* Marsh samphire is part of the goosefoot family (Chenopodiaceae). The plant forms a part of many studies into the ecology of marginal marine environments but it has not been examined for any potential pharmaceutical benefits.

## Red Valerian – *Centranthus ruber*

'It is warm and aromatic, of a rather fetid smell.'

Henry Philips, 1829

- Etymology: Greek, *kentros*, a spur; *anthos*, a flower
- Perennial; on chalky ground and walls across southern Britain but especially in coastal regions. Numerous flowers, red or white in heads; leaves ovate.

Although mentioned in the fifteenth-century works of Chaucer, red valerian is an introduced garden plant which has escaped into the countryside where it may be found on alkaline soils or growing along the tops of walls (often in profusion). In the springtime it produces a beautiful red or white flower but it is the young leaves which are edible, although their bitter flavour will not be to everyone's taste.

*Cookery:* Red valerian leaves and root are edible but both have a bitter taste and in my opinion it is better to ignore the root in favour of the young, fresh leaves which may be picked in the springtime. Washed leaves may be used raw in salads, but do so sparingly, or part-boiled and served as a side vegetable. The root has traditionally been washed, chopped and boiled to form a part of broths and soups but, as with the leaves, it should be used only as a minor ingredient (see Introduction regarding the uprooting of wild plants).

*Historical Uses:* It was the roots of red valerian that were principally used by apothecaries; these would typically be gathered in the early spring, before the plant began growing vigorously. Principally used to treat disorders of the nervous system, red valerian was also said to benefit eyesight and was at one time fed to horses to preserve or even enhance their vision. In more recent times valerian has been used as a treatment for insomnia and fatigue (see below).

*Scientific Notes:* Red valerian is a member of the valerian family (Valerianaceae). Analysis reveals valerian to have some sedative properties and it is recommended that those who are to undergo surgery should not regularly consume the plant (or its extracts) for several weeks beforehand. Those who are taking other forms of sedative or antidepressant drugs should probably avoid regular consumption. Valerian's active compounds include isovalerianic, formic, acetic acids and pinene.

## Rock Samphire – *Crithmum maritimum*

'Nor untrembling canst thou see,
How from a craggy rock, whose prominence
Half overshades the ocean, hardy men.
Fearless of rending winds and dashing waves,
Cut Sampire, to excite the squeamish gust
Of pamper'd luxury.'

Henry Philips, 1829

- Alternative Names: Golden Samphire, Marine Fennel, Sea Fennel
- Etymology: Greek, *krithe*, barley, from the shape of its fruit
- Perennial; coastal regions across the British Isles except northern Scotland. Flowers yellowish in umbels; fleshy, narrow leaves; smells aromatic.

Rock samphire is sometimes confused in historical literature with marsh samphire (*q.v.*), but it is a very different plant which lives on shingle banks, cliff faces, harbour walls and other rocky coastal habitats. At one time rock samphire was commercially gathered for sale in marketplaces. The poem above refers to the hazards many samphire gatherers would endure to reach the best plants on rock faces and cliff tops.

*Cookery:* Rock samphire stems and fleshy leaves are edible and possess an aromatic, peppery taste. The plant is at its most flavoursome during the spring, before it flowers, but it may be harvested throughout the summer as well.

Historically rock samphire was a popular vegetable that, if fresh enough, would sometimes be eaten raw in salads where it adds a fresh, peppery taste. The leaves would, however, more commonly be boiled or steamed and eaten as greens, especially with meat dishes. The sixteenth-century herbalist Gerard commented: 'The leaves kept in pickle, and eaten in salads with oil and vinegar, is a pleasant sauce for meat, and stirreth up an appetite to meat.'

The plant was also used to garnish some fish dishes and could be pickled in an identical manner to marsh samphire. I have also used rock samphire by blanching the leaves in boiling water for a couple of minutes, then adding as an ingredient in seafood risotto and pasta.

*Historical Uses:* Regarded as being 'more used by the cook than the apothecary', rock samphire had few hard and fast uses in herbalist treatments. Culpeper said of it: 'It is a safe herb, very pleasant both to taste and stomach, helpeth digestion, and in some sort opening obstructions of the liver and spleen; provoketh urine, and helpeth thereby to wash away the gravel and stone engendered in the kidneys or bladder.'

*Scientific Notes:* Rock samphire is a member of the carrot family (Apiaceae). The plant has notable concentrations of antioxidants and it has antimicrobial properties, but no specific health benefits have been associated with it.

## Scurvygrass – *Cochlearia officinalis; C. danica*

'It is the general opinion that the taste be not so agreeable.'

John Hill, 1812

- Etymology: Latin, *cochlear*, a spoon, from the shape of its leaves
- Perennial; all British Isles, mostly coastal. Flower white with four petals; leaves small, fleshy and rounded.

Scurvygrass is a common coastal plant and gets its common name from it having allegedly having been eaten by returning sailors suffering from a lack of fresh fruit and vegetables in their diet. There are several related and similar-looking species in the British Isles, all of which are edible. Scurvygrass is a low, spreading plant that may be hidden by other larger plants. It is most easily seen when growing on coastal walls, cliffs or salt marshes and, although essentially maritime, the plant also occurs inland on mountains and along the verge of motorways. The leaves may be gathered in the spring and summer and are eaten raw but they possess a sharp, acrid taste (derived from the plant's levels of oxalic acid) that will perhaps not suit some modern palates.

*Cookery:* The leaves of scurvygrass are small and fleshy but the overpowering taste means that you will not need to gather many of them. Those wishing to use this plant would do well to pick the leaves in the spring, before the plant flowers, when they are young and fresh. To use simply wash and then add (sparingly) to salads or as a garnish.

Rock samphire (p. 168).

Scurvygrass (p. 169).

Sea beet (opposite).

*Historical Uses:* The main herbalist use for scurvygrass was as an antiscorbutic (i.e. to prevent scurvy), the prescription for which was either to eat the leaves raw or to extract the juice which would often be added to apple or orange juice to make it more palatable. It was also said to be helpful in cases of rheumatism and 'foulness of the blood'.

*Scientific Notes:* Scurvygrass is part of the cabbage family (Brassicaceae). As its common name suggests, scurvygrass is a noted antiscorbutic plant although it has been observed that, contrary to historical medical advice, eating this plant alone is not sufficient to stave off the disease. Excessive consumption of scurvygrass has been linked to a degeneration in eyesight and the plant's seed also contains low levels of goitrogen compounds, which suppresses the thyroid gland. There is, however, no evidence to suggest that scurvygrass is detrimental to the health.

## Sea Beet – *Beta vulgaris* subsp. *maritima*

> 'Its leaves, when dressed, are extremely delicate and well-flavoured, and easily reduced into that pulpy substance which constitutes the great merit of good spinach.'
>
> *The Penny 'Cyclopaedia*, 1835

- Etymology: Latin/Celtic, *beta*, food
- Perennial; All British coasts except north Scotland. Flower green in spikes; leaves broad, fleshy and long-stemmed.

Sea beet is a very common and distinctive coastal plant that may be found growing in clumps on walls, cliffs and beach-top verges, usually within reach of the sea. Sea beet is believed to be the wild ancestor of modern commercial plants such as sugar beet and beetroot. It produces lengthy, fleshy leaves, the youngest and most tender of which may be picked throughout the spring and summer (older leaves can be tough and bitter). The cooked leaves taste very much like spinach and are popular, even among non-foragers, making sea beet one of the more famous edible coastal plants.

*Cookery:* The leaves of sea beet were once widely eaten in the same manner as spinach, being picked, washed, cut into thin lengths and then boiled for several minutes until soft. This remains their greatest use but the leaves can also be added to soups and stews and wrapped around broiled poultry and fish. More modern uses include making it an ingredient for stir-fries and curries.

*SEA BEET SOUP (based on an 1823 recipe)*
Chop one onion and fry it in a good knob of melted butter. Add 1000ml of vegetable stock and bring to the boil. Wash two generous handfuls of sea beet; chop and add this to the stock. Add seasoning (which might include small amounts of wild fennel or rock samphire). Simmer for about 10 mins, until all the ingredients are soft, then liquidise. Eat

at once or allow to cool and keep in the fridge (it also freezes well). For a thicker soup, add a couple of potatoes with the sea beet and cook until soft.

*Historical Uses:* The leaves of all the common beet plants were at one time prescribed as a laxative and were also said to have emollient qualities. The leaves, if softened with a hot iron and then soaked in beer, would be applied to the skin in cases of blistering, ulceration and minor scalds. However, the medicinal uses of beet had all but disappeared by the eighteenth century, it being favoured as an edible vegetable.

*Scientific Notes:* Sea beet is part of the goosefoot family (Chenopodiaceae). This plant is notably high in antioxidants and roughage but it does not appear to have been studied in relation to any health or medical benefits. Some studies note that the plant has a resistance to certain herbicides, which leads to the possibility that it could survive in areas which have been sprayed with weedkillers; make sure that any leaves are well washed before cooking!

### Sea Kale – *Crambe maritima*

- Alternative Names: Sea Cale, Colewort
- Etymology: Greek, *crambe*, a cabbage
- Perennial; much of coastal British Isles, except northern Scotland. Tends to be localised. White flowers; broad, fleshy leaves.

Sea kale had long been a popular dish in Ireland but was ignored in Britain until 1767 when a Dr Lettsom began to cultivate it in his garden. Lettsom expounded its culinary virtues to others, including the Bishop of Carlisle, and the plant was further popularised by a 1799 discourse written by London doctor William Curtis. It is the asparagus-like quality of sea kale (and its ascribed medical qualities, see below) that has attracted so much attention and which, prior to the Great War, led to many coasts being stripped bare of their plants.

The plant should be picked during the spring, when the shoots begin to push their way through the sand and shingle in which it commonly lives. It has a strong taste that is reminiscent of spinach.

*Cookery:* In Victorian times the demand was such that wild sea kale was in short supply and so the plant would be cultivated in gardens or small commercial plots. It could be found on sale at most marketplaces, but by the turn of the twentieth century sea kale's popularity had faded so that these days it is rarely eaten.

Shoots should be harvested in the springtime using a knife. Find a plant and keep an eye on it; cut the shoots as soon as they start to appear and ideally when they are still blanched white. (The older shoots can be tough and bitter.) Make sure that you do not denude the plant of all its young shoots, and wash them thoroughly.

The best means of preparing sea kale shoots is to treat them like asparagus: trim away any woody material from the shoots and place them in boiling water for a few minutes.

When tender, remove and serve with melted butter and lemon juice or hollandaise sauce. In most respects blanched sea kale may act as a substitute for asparagus in recipes; I have, for example, used it in green risottos and various pasta dishes.

*DRESSED SEA KALE (1843 recipe)*
Tie the sea-kale shoots in bundles, and boil it in plenty of water, with a little salt in it, for twenty minutes. Observe that the water is boiling before it is put in. Have a piece of toast ready, dip it in the water, put it on the serving dish and place the sea-kale upon it. Pour a little white sauce over it, consisting of an equal quantity of veal gravy, and cream thickened with flour and butter. If desired, a less rich sauce may be made by leaving out the gravy, and substituting milk for the cream.

*Historical Uses:* It was William Curtis who started a craze for sea kale when he afforded the plant miraculous health-giving properties, including an ability to 'sweeten the blood'. Curtis's faith was such that he believed eating the vegetable in spring would keep the doctor away: 'I grow my own medicine,' wrote he. Prior to the time of Curtis, the plant would seem to have been generally overlooked by herbalists.

*Scientific Notes:* Sea kale is part of the cabbage family (Brassicaceae). The plant contains relatively high levels of glucosinolates, chemical compounds that are toxic in large doses (they may cause thyroid problems) but which, in smaller amounts, have been linked to health benefits, including cancer prevention. Glucosinolates are destroyed by prolonged cooking and are also found in a variety of vegetables including broccoli, cauliflower and brussels sprouts.

## Sea Purslane – *Atriplex portulacoides*

- Alternative Name: Shrubby Orache
- Etymology: Greek, *a*, not; *trephein*, nourishing
- Perennial; strictly coastal around England, Wales, Ireland and southern Scotland. Flowers pale yellow in spikes; leaves fleshy, oval with silvery shine.

Sea purslane is a distinctive, shrubby plant that is restricted to soils located just above the high tide mark, usually within reach of the sea's spray. The plant is most often associated with salt marsh environments but it may also be found growing behind artificial barriers such as sea walls, where the ground gets periodically drenched by the waves. The plant is little remarked upon historically and does not appear to have been widely eaten.

It is sea purslane's young leaves that are edible, raw or cooked; these have an attractive silvery hue and may be gathered throughout the year, but are at their best in the spring and summer. They have a strong, salty, vegetable taste.

*Cookery:* Sea purslane does not feature widely in historical cookbooks, although it was remarked upon as being edible in some gardening dictionaries. The leaves are the only

**Above and right:** *Sea kale (p. 172).*

*Sea purslane (p. 173).*

palatable part of the plant and you should choose the healthiest, succulent-looking ones. Thoroughly wash the leaves as they may accumulate sand and grit from the sea shore.

The traditional way of eating sea purslane is to blanch the leaves in boiling water for several minutes, until soft. They can then be drained and served as a side vegetable with butter and pepper. The blanched leaves can be liquidised with other herbs, such as parsley, and be used as a dressing for fish dishes; the raw leaves may also be added to the stock when cooking shellfish such as mussels and clams. The cooked leaves may also be chopped and incorporated into other dishes such as pasta, risotto and warm salads.

*Historical Uses:* I can find little historical reference to the use of sea purslane in herbalist preparations, although it is remarked upon that the plant is a good source of alkaloid salts. In general terms the leaves of sea purslane and other members of the genus *Atriplex* are said to be effective when applied to bruises and, more remarkably, are said to be able to reduce the prominence of a sticking-out navel in children.

*Scientific Notes:* Sea purslane is part of the goosefoot family (Chenopodiaceae). It is an ecologically important plant and as such it has been widely studied by botanists and environmental scientists. It has not, however, been studied with regard to any potential health or medicinal properties.

## Wild Cabbage – *Brassica oleracea*

'Wild cabbage is as delicious a vegetable as I ever eat.'
Letter to *Gardener's Magazine*, 1831

- Alternative Names: Sea Cabbage, Sea Colewort
- Etymology: Celtic, *bresic*, a pottage made from this plant
- Perennial; a locally common coastal species from all the British Isles that may occasionally be found growing inland. Yellow flowers in heads; leaves fleshy, oblong and wavy.

*Wild cabbage.*

Wild cabbage has been eaten for centuries and was considered by some urban chefs to hold a superior flavour to the domesticated variety. Although, as more than one historical horticulturalist has noted, the plant was not held in similar esteem by country folk and would often be ignored or even shunned by them.

The wild cabbage is most often associated with lime-rich soils and in Victorian times the plant was a notable feature of the white cliffs of Dover and other chalk headlands. It may also be found on coastal waste ground and is known from some inland locations, especially in southern England. It is the young, fleshy leaves that are gathered, generally in the early spring, when they are most tender. They taste like cabbage (not surprisingly).

*Cookery:* Historically wild cabbage was not widely used as a food source and there are a number of early Victorian commentators who express surprise at the populace's general ignorance of the plant.

Pick healthy, young leaves in the early spring and wash well. They are best treated as though they are normal cabbage and should be cut or shredded, then boiled in water for a few minutes until tender. They may then be served as a side dish for a variety of main courses. Equally well, the plant may be directly substituted for garden cabbage in almost any cookbook recipe and is particularly good when used as part of a vegetable soup.

Historical variations include an insistence that wild cabbage be cooked using two changes of water or that it should be boiled in milk. There are also references to the leaves being dried and then added to winter soups. Older leaves would be wrapped around fish and broiled.

*Historical Uses:* The localised occurrence of the wild cabbage meant that it was not widely used by apothecaries except as a substitute for domesticated cabbage and some other similarly related brassicas. Nicholas Culpeper claimed that wild cabbage, if made into a broth, would cleanse the digestive system of parasites and that the leaves could help heal wounds and skin diseases.

*Scientific Notes:* Wild cabbage is part of the cabbage family (Brassicaceae). In common with several other related vegetables (e.g. cauliflower), wild cabbage has been tentatively cited as helping in the prevention of cancer although this has yet to be absolutely proven. It is generally high in antioxidants and roughage and is acknowledged to be healthy when eaten as part of a balanced diet.

## Sea Carrot/Wild Carrot – *Daucus carota*

> 'By what accident this plant, with its slender fusiform root, has been changed into the plant of our gardens, is unknown.'
>
> David Low, 1834

- Alternative Names: Bishop's Lace, Bird's Nest
- Etymology: Greek, *Daucus*, the old name for this plant
- Perennial; coastal dunes and dry grasslands in southern British Isles. Flowers white in large umbel; the central flower is red-purple.

Wild carrot is a widespread plant but it is more common in coastal regions than elsewhere. In southern regions the plant has a fleshier-leaved maritime variety known as sea carrot (*D. carota* subsp. *gummifer*) which, it should be noted, is listed as being in decline nationally. The roots of wild carrot are small, knobbly and frequently woody, all of which serves to make it a plant which is ignored by all but the most dedicated of foragers. It should be foraged for in the autumn months.

Like some other members of the carrot family, the plant's sap may irritate or even burn the skin, so consider wearing gloves when dealing with it; there is also a resemblance to members of the **highly poisonous hemlock family** so check your identification!

*Cookery:* Wild carrots may be found growing in coastal dunes (usually as the variety called sea carrot) or in dry, chalky grasslands. Some of these areas are ecologically sensitive and may even be protected, so please think of the local environment before digging up swathes of land. The carrot plant should be dug up in the autumn or early winter; it is best to ignore the larger plants in favour of the medium-sized ones, as the roots may be fleshier and less woody. It may take a while to find enough roots to make up a meal (see Introduction regarding the uprooting of wild plants).

In the kitchen the roots should be thoroughly scrubbed and any imperfections scraped or cut out. They may then be treated in much the same manner as a farmed carrot and boiled/steamed for a few minutes to form a vegetable side dish. Other traditional uses include the preparation of carrot juice by cutting up the roots, then beating them to a pulp and expressing the juice through a sieve. This method was sometimes also used to form a traditional carrot soup.

*CARROT SOUP (adapted from an 1826 recipe)*
Take at least a dozen or more carrot roots which have been cleaned and cut thin. If you cannot muster up this number of carrots then add some turnip to make up the volume. Finely cut and in a large saucepan fry two onions in olive oil/butter. Add the carrots and a generous amount of vegetable or beef stock (about 500ml) and stew them till soft enough to pulp using a blender. Add another 500ml of stock and boil until slightly thickened. (According to the original recipe it is to be 'as thick as peas soup'.) Season with salt, pepper

Wild carrot (p. 177).

Sea carrot (p. 177).

and cayenne. The original recipe recommends letting the soup stand for a day before reheating and serving, but this really isn't necessary.

*Historical Uses:* It was the seeds of the wild carrot plant that were most commonly used in herbalist preparations where they were said to help with indigestion, flatulence and other minor digestive disorders. Nicholas Culpeper also comments that the plant helps increase fertility, something which is at odds with its use in ancient Greece and Rome as a contraceptive. The leaves were said to have been used with honey as a dressing for wounds and ulcers, and the expressed juice as a cure for intestinal parasites.

*Scientific Notes:* Wild carrot is part of the carrot family (Apiaceae). Laboratory tests using sea carrot suggest that the plant may assist in protecting the liver and could even help this organ in recovery from injury. Extracts from sea carrot seeds have been tested for use as a possible herbal contraceptive as they apparently disrupt the egg implantation process.

*Chapter Seven*

# Seaweeds

In Britain there are very few plants which can tolerate prolonged immersion in seawater (seagrass being a notable exception but it is utterly inedible) and so the forager on the seashore must make use of marine algae (i.e. seaweed). There is no shortage of seaweed on most British coasts but like all organisms, there are some areas in which it grows better than others. Rocky coastlines are usually the best place as these offer hard surfaces to which the seaweed can anchor itself and flourish; also seaweed growing on rocks is less likely to have sand, bits of shell and other crunchy particles trapped in it. Seaweed will be found on sandy shores but it can be of an inferior quality.

Seaweeds grow in distinct zones on the beach with the greatest variety occurring on the lower part of the shore (i.e. the part uncovered for the least time at low tide). When foraging for seaweed try to pick a 'spring tide' (when the tidal range is greatest) as this will offer you the greatest exposure of intertidal area. Head onto the beach about one to two hours before the time of low water and work your way along the lower shore. At the

*Rocky shores are a forager's dream.*

time of low water, stop and start working your way back up towards dry land: do not be tempted to linger. The tide may rise in unexpected ways, cutting you off and leading to the risk of drowning or the drama of a lifeboat rescue. Always consult a tide table before taking to the seashore or its associated environments and forage on a falling tide, not a rising one.

Other hazards include: a risk of getting wet and becoming cold; slippery surfaces (especially those covered in seaweed); and hostile animals such as crabs and conger eels hiding among the rocks. Also, be wary of getting stuck in mud which may be a problem in marshes, estuaries and harbours. Keep a watch for any potential sources of pollution and be especially careful of foraging close to outfalls which may carry sewage or stream water which contains input from farms. Even the cleanest-looking of beaches may be harbouring nasty bacteria and viruses (e.g. *E. coli*) that have been transported there from several miles away. Harbours, marinas and industrially developed stretches of coast carry a risk of chemical pollution (e.g. antifouling and oil). If in doubt, ask locals for their opinion on the water quality.

Spring and early summer are the best times to collect seaweeds as they are growing vigorously and will be relatively free of encrusting organisms. Choose fresh-looking patches which, if possible, are growing above any sediment, such as sand. As with terrestrial plants, harvest seaweeds sustainably by cutting them a few centimetres above the holdfast (root) that attaches it to the rock. This will allow them to grow again. When you get the seaweed home, soak it in fresh water for at least twenty minutes: this will kill most clinging animals, such as amphipods and small sea snails. Then rinse it thoroughly to get rid of any sand and dirt.

### *DRYING SEAWEED*

Traditionally, seaweed is gathered and then dried for later use. This is best done in warm weather when it can be spread outside on a clean blanket or tarpaulin and left for a few days to dry out (turn the seaweed fronds over once or twice). Failing this, place the seaweed on a tray in an oven on a low heat and leave until crispy and brittle. When completely dry the plants may be stored in an airtight container for up to a year.

### *DEEP-FRIED SEAWEED*

I probably ought to confess that despite my love of the seashore, I am not actually very fond of eating seaweed (although I know many people who love it). However, there is one method of cooking seaweed which is guaranteed to delight all comers, of whatever taste and age, and that is to deep-fry it. All the seaweeds covered in this chapter (plus several other species not covered here such as the oarweed species; e.g. *Laminaria digitata*) may be deep-fried to create a delicious crispy snack or to form an hors d'œuvre as part of a Chinese meal.

To accomplish this, get a deep fat fryer or place some oil in a large saucepan or wok (do not overfill) and heat until smoking. Wash the seaweed and squeeze as much water out of it as possible; in the case of larger seaweeds, cut into smaller clumps or strips. Add a small handful at a time and cook for no more than a few seconds before removing and drying on absorbent paper. Watch out for spitting. The resultant crispy mass is wonderful and may be eaten as a snack or used as a garnish for salads and soups.

## Carragheen – *Chondrus crispus*

> 'It is the best thickener of milk, broths, etc., makes excellent jellies, and for Blanche-Mange is equal to most expensive ingredients, whilst the cost is comparatively nothing.'
>
> *Mechanics' Magazine*, 1835

- Alternative Name: Irish Moss
- Attached to rocks on the lower shore; common on the western and southern coasts of the British Isles.

Carragheen can be found attached to lower shore rocks where it may be abundant. Its use as a gelling and thickening agent is well-known especially in Ireland, where it has been particularly popular as a food source, but it is also used commercially. There was a general revival in the domestic use of carragheen after rationing was imposed during World War Two, while the recent rise of vegetarianism has seen it appear in many health food shops.

Carragheen may be gathered at any time but the best results come from young fronds harvested in the spring which may be dried for later use. Carragheen has a resemblance to another seaweed (*Mastocarpus stellatus*), but the latter has curled edges along the stems and fronds.

*Cookery:* Dried carragheen may be bought from some health food shops but it is a simple enough task to make your own version. Pick a quantity of the seaweed and rinse it well before leaving it to soak in fresh water for around twenty minutes or so: this kills any small sea creatures and generally improves the flavour. Remove from the water and lay out the fronds on a tray (or similar) in a place where it will dry naturally (e.g. in a sheltered location outdoors, in a shed or airing cupboard, etc.). When absolutely dry, store in a sealed container until needed.

To cook carragheen, simply place the washed or dried weed into a saucepan of water and boil until dissolved into a viscous mass (this may take some hours). This mixture may be used neat as a gelling agent in various dessert dishes and as a thickening agent in soups, ice creams, etc.

*CARRAGHEEN BLANCMANGE AND JELLIES (based on an 1835 recipe)*
Take 15g of carragheen, and having cleansed it, boil it in 800ml of new milk, until it is reduced to a proper thickness to retain its shape. Sweeten and flavour with lemon, white wine, or anything to suit the palate. To make Orange, Lemon or Savoury jellies: use a

*Carragheen (p. 181).*

similar process, substituting water for milk – add lemon, orange, herbs, etc. according to taste.

*CARRAGHEEN BREAKFAST DRINK*

Historically a nutritious breakfast drink would be made by boiling a few grams of carragheen in milk until a thickened mixture results, after which honey or sugar would be added to sweeten.

*Historical Uses:* For centuries carragheen has been recognised to have general health-giving properties and to be easily digestible. Concentrated mixtures would be given to people (especially infants) suffering from undernourishment or those with diet-related ailments such as rickets, dysentery and scurvy. Gelatinous sweets of carragheen would be used to assuage coughs and sore throats.

*Scientific Notes:* Carragheen is a red seaweed, extracts from which (mostly polysaccharides such as agar and carragheenin) are used in many products, including food and medicines.

*Purple laver.*

The annual value of seaweed crops in the USA is around $6 billion, but products have been linked to allergic reactions in some people. There appear to be few studies on the pharmaceutical benefits of carragheen, although it is generally viewed as being a healthy product.

## Purple Laver – *Porphyra umbilicalis*

> 'It is seldom liked at first, but people become extremely fond of it by habit.'
>
> Maria Rundell, 1824

- Alternative Name: Laver
- Common on rocky shores around the British Isles.

Clumps of limp, purplish-black laver adorn rocks on the middle and lower seashore (it occurs on the upper shore but I prefer to gather it further down). Historically laver was not so widely eaten as carragheen but it has become popular recently in the form of laverbread, a traditional dish from southern Wales (Welsh: *bara lawr*). It is not difficult to find on rocky shores and should be gathered during the early spring and dried for later use.

*Cookery:* Like carragheen, laver breaks down into a gelatinous mass on cooking but it is resistant and the end result is not as versatile as a gelling agent, although it may be used as a general thickener for soups.

*LAVERBREAD*

Laver's most famous incarnation is as laverbread which originates from Glamorgan, Wales, the recipe for which also provides a general method for the preparation of laver. First the seaweed must be thoroughly rinsed and cleaned of any animals, sand, etc., and then placed in a heavy pan filled with cold water. Bring this to a simmer and cook for an extended period of anywhere between four and six hours, stirring and topping up the water as necessary. Once the seaweed has broken into small pieces, strain off any remaining water then use a hand blender to create a green-black paste. This should be cooled afterwards and may be stored in the fridge for several days.

Laverbread (also known as 'the Welshman's caviar') is often eaten in this purėed form (hot and cold), spread on toast or sometimes in accompaniment to fish, shellfish or lamb. Laverbread may also be used to flavour a variety of other dishes, such as risotto, soups and gravies.

An alternative use for laverbread is as a breakfast cake, whereupon the purée is tipped into a bowl containing a handful of oatmeal and rolled about until fully coated. It is then fried in a pan (traditionally in bacon fat but butter or oil will do) and served with bacon or scrambled eggs.

*LAVER SAUCE (1824 recipe)*

Set some laver on a dish over heat, with a bit of butter, and the squeeze of an orange. Stir it till hot. It is eaten with roast meat, and is a great sweetener of the blood.

*Historical Uses:* There are few historical references to laver as having been afforded specifically medicinal properties. However, and like many seaweeds, it was thought of as a generally healthy food which could be given to the infirm or those suffering from dietary problems.

*Scientific Notes:* Laver is a red seaweed whose properties are similar to those of carragheen (see this entry for details).

## Dulse – *Palmaria palmata*

> 'Without undergoing the least preparation, dulse is much eaten and relished by the poor people, to whom a large handful is sold for a penny.'
>
> John Carr, 1809

- Common on rocky shores all round the British Isles.

Deemed as utterly inedible by some, dried dulse was once commonly sold at street markets, especially in Scotland and Ireland, where this seaweed was much valued as a food. It is certainly chewy and moist when eaten raw, but the texture can be transformed by drying or cooking. It is at its best in the spring and summer when it should be looked for during spring tides at low water.

Dulse should not be confused with *Dilsea carnosa* ('red rags') which looks similar but is less edible (although Cornishmen were said to pinch its fronds between hot irons, which allegedly gives it the taste of a cooked oyster).

*Cookery:* Dulse may be found on rocks on the lower shore and reaches an edible size in the late spring and summer. It may be eaten raw from the shore as a vegetable or in salads but it benefits from being either dried or cooked, which helps tenderise its toughness. To dry dulse, thoroughly wash the fronds then lay out in a sheltered, convenient place and allow to naturally dehydrate, perhaps turning once or twice. To re-animate, soak in warm water for several minutes.

In addition to being eaten raw, dulse may be boiled or steamed until tender and served with butter; it may also be deep-fried briefly until it becomes crispy. Those who would like to add a taste of the sea to their soups, chowders, etc., can put in a small amount of dulse during cooking or, if the seaweed itself is not wanted, they can soak it in hot water, then use the resultant strained liquid.

*Historical Uses:* 'Dulse will cure all maladies except black death.' This was the historical opinion of the coastal Norwegians, some of whom insisted that their general wellbeing was dependent on the seaweed. Like other seaweeds, the concentrated nutritional value of dulse has led to it being viewed as a health food, but there are instances of the seaweed being administered to those suffering from high fevers.

*Scientific Notes:* Dulse is a red seaweed that has been linked to cancer prevention, with laboratory tests suggesting that there may be a 'casual link' between extracts from the plant and a reduced risk of breast and intestinal tumours. Extracts from dulse have a wide commercial use (see entry for carragheen).

Dulse (p. 185).

Sea lettuce (opposite).

## Sea Lettuce – *Ulva lactuca*

> 'It has within a few years been introduced to fashionable tables, being stewed with lemon juice.'
>
> James Smith, 1803

- Alternative Names: Green Laver, Oyster Green
- Common on rocky and stony shores, especially on the upper shore.

Sea lettuce was probably a long-standing food source among coastal communities but for reasons unknown in the eighteenth century it briefly became fashionable on the dinner tables of the well-to-do before fading into obscurity again. It has a bitter taste but this seaweed does make a good addition to salads and soups. It can be harvested in the spring and summer months.

*Cookery:* Sea lettuce is easy to find on most stony and rocky shores but it may be preferable to gather it from off the rocks away from sandy areas, as the seaweed has a habit of trapping particles among its folds. It may also thrive close to outfalls and other potential sources of man-made pollution, so it may be wise to take local advice before heading down to the beach. Choose the youngest, freshest-looking plants and cut it away from the rock using a knife.

At home the sea lettuce must be thoroughly rinsed and cleaned in fresh water to remove all sand, etc. It may be stored in the fridge for two days, kept frozen for four months or dried in the sun and stored as crispy sheets.

Fresh sea lettuce may be eaten raw but it is best prepared by chopping roughly then lightly steaming or frying it for a few minutes. In this state it may be used as a side vegetable (with butter, lemon juice or flavoured vinegar) or as a salad component. It may also be added raw to soups, broths and chowders. One may also wrap fish in it or add it to stir-fries.

*Historical Uses:* Sea lettuce was sometimes prescribed for those suffering from scrofula ('the King's evil') or scurvy and was known as a general health food. In 1798 George Shaw acknowledged its medical benefits but complained that it 'can scarcely be taken in sufficient quantities to do much good, without too strong an effect on the bowels'.

*Scientific Notes:* Sea lettuce is a fast-growing green seaweed that responds quickly to increased nutrient levels in sea water. In recent years this has caused problems in areas where effluent is discharged into the sea or where streams and rivers bring in high levels of nitrates and phosphates. The sea lettuce responds to the heightened nutrient levels by forming dense growths across the seashore; these eventually start to rot releasing hydrogen sulphide gas, the smell of which upsets tourists and locals alike. In 2009 rotting sea lettuce was blamed for the death of a horse in Brittany, France, when it was rendered unconscious by the fumes. Steroids extracted from sea lettuce have been assessed as having potential anti-inflammatory properties.

## *Chapter Eight*

# The Forager's Calendar

Below is a calendar demonstrating when in the year particular plants may best be foraged for. Given the wide geographical extent of the British Isles (which stretches from the boreal Orkney Islands to the temperate Channel Islands), the seasons arrive at different times and are of different duration. This is important as plants use the weather and levels of daylight to control their growth, flowering and fruiting. Bear this in mind when looking at the list below.

Generally speaking, the further south and west you are, the earlier the spring and summer weather will be, with the winter weather arriving later and being of less severity. Proximity to the sea and elevation will also affect the annual cycle of plants.

### Winter

The winter months (December to March) offer little light and heat and so the majority of plants will die back and become dormant. Consequently winter is a lean time for the forager but there are a few autumn fruits, roots and hardy plants that can be gathered and eaten. Many foragers will prepare for winter by drying or preserving summer fruits and herbs so that come December their larder is well stocked.

| Plant Name | Chapter | Page No. |
|---|---|---|
| Biting Stonecrop | Garden | 45 |
| Blackthorn (sloes) | Hedge | 56 |
| Chickweed | Garden | 33 |
| Common Wintercress | Hedge | 75 |
| Crowberry | Grassland | 140 |
| Dandelion | Garden | 36 |
| Horseradish | Hedge | 66 |
| Medlar | Hedge | 88 |
| Rosemary | Garden | 39 |
| Sea Purslane | Coastal | 173 |
| Watercress | Wetlands | 154 |
| Wild Parsnips | Grassland | 147 |

## Spring

As the dark days and low temperatures of winter give way to the warmth and light of spring (March to May), so the choice of plants increases greatly. The period following Easter is probably the best time of the year for foraging as many plants will have awakened and be pushing out lots of tender young leaves and shoots while others will start to come into flower. It is a joy to see the hedgerows and fields coming to life, changing week by week until they become a positive riot of plant life, fighting for space and light.

| Plant Name | Chapter | Page No. |
|---|---|---|
| Alexanders | Coastal | 160 |
| Bistort | Hedge | 80 |
| Biting Stonecrop | Garden | 45 |
| Black Mustard | Coastal | 161 |
| Borage | Garden | 29 |
| Broom | Forest | 115 |
| Burdock | Garden | 31 |
| Carragheen | Seaweed | 181 |
| Catmint/catnip | Grassland | 145 |
| Chamomile | Grassland | 124 |
| Chickweed | Garden | 33 |
| Cleavers | Hedge | 57 |
| Coltsfoot | Garden | 34 |
| Comfrey | Wetlands | 156 |
| Common Sorrel | Hedge | 60 |
| Common Wintercress | Hedge | 75 |
| Corn Salad | Grassland | 127 |
| Cow Parsley | Hedge | 76 |
| Dandelion | Garden | 36 |
| Dulse | Seaweed | 185 |
| Elder | Forest | 101 |
| Fat Hen | Hedge | 84 |
| Garlic Mustard | Hedge | 61 |
| Good King Henry | Hedge | 83 |
| Gorse | Grassland | 128 |
| Ground Elder | Garden | 37 |
| Ground Ivy | Hedge | 63 |
| Hairy Bittercress | Garden | 41 |
| Hogweed | Forest | 113 |
| Ivy-Leaved Toadflax | Garden | 43 |

| | | |
|---|---|---|
| Lady's Smock | Wetlands | 152 |
| Laver | Seaweed | 183 |
| Lime | Forest | 52 |
| Mallow | Coastal | 164 |
| Marsh Samphire | Coastal | 165 |
| Meadowsweet | Wetlands | 153 |
| Mugwort | Hedge | 85 |
| Nettles | Garden | 49 |
| Pignut | Forest | 111 |
| Plantain | Garden | 44 |
| Primrose | Hedge | 68 |
| Ramsons | Forest | 100 |
| Rape | Hedge | 161 |
| Red Dead Nettle | Garden | 48 |
| Red Goosefoot | Garden | 84 |
| Red Valerian | Coastal | 167 |
| Rock Samphire | Coastal | 168 |
| Rosebay Willowherb | Garden | 47 |
| Rosemary | Garden | 39 |
| Salad Burnet | Grassland | 131 |
| Scurvy Grass | Coastal | 169 |
| Sea Beet | Coastal | 171 |
| Sea Kale | Coastal | 172 |
| Sea Lettuce | Seaweed | 187 |
| Sea Purslane | Coastal | 173 |
| Silverweed | Hedge | 89 |
| Smooth Sow Thistle | Grassland | 132 |
| Sweet Cicely | Hedge | 79 |
| Tansy | Hedge | 69 |
| Three-Cornered Garlic | Hedge | 77 |
| Wall Pennywort | Garden | 40 |
| Watercress | Wetlands | 154 |
| White Dead Nettle | Garden | 48 |
| Wild Basil | Grassland | 137 |
| Wild Cabbage | Coastal | 175 |
| Wild Hops | Hedge | 71 |
| Wild Marjoram | Grassland | 135 |
| Wood Avens | Forest | 105 |
| Woodruff | Forest | 112 |
| Yarrow | Grassland | 133 |

## Summer

The summer (June to August) is eagerly anticipated in Britain and the arrival of a week or so of sunshine can lighten the nation's mood remarkably. For foragers it is an odd season that roughly speaking is split into the earlier months, which tend to receive an overspill of edible plants from the spring, and the later months, which see the first of the autumn fruits start to ripen. It is a wonderful time for foraging, not least because many people will take the family on holiday to exciting parts of the country which will offer access to a different variety of plants. It is also a time when the forager should begin to think of the winter by drying herbs, seaweeds, etc., and making preserves with the first of the autumn fruits.

| Plant Name | Chapter | Page No. |
|---|---|---|
| Agrimony | Hedge | 53 |
| Bilberry | Grassland | 121 |
| Biting Stonecrop | Garden | 45 |
| Bog Myrtle | Wetlands | 151 |
| Borage | Garden | 29 |
| Burdock | Garden | 31 |
| Carragheen | Seaweed | 181 |
| Catmint/catnip | Grassland | 145 |
| Chamomile | Grassland | 124 |
| Chickweed | Garden | 33 |
| Cleavers | Hedge | 57 |
| Cranberry | Wetlands | 157 |
| Dandelion | Garden | 36 |
| Dulse | Seaweed | 185 |
| Fat Hen | Hedge | 84 |
| Fennel | Coastal | 163 |
| Garlic Mustard | Hedge | 61 |
| Good King Henry | Hedge | 83 |
| Ground Ivy | Hedge | 63 |
| Hairy Bittercress | Garden | 41 |
| Heather | Grassland | 129 |
| Hogweed | Forest | 113 |
| Ivy-Leaved Toadflax | Garden | 43 |
| Laver | Seaweed | 183 |
| Marsh Samphire | Coastal | 165 |
| Meadowsweet | Wetlands | 153 |
| Mugwort | Hedge | 85 |

| | | |
|---|---|---|
| Plantain | Garden | 44 |
| Poppy | Grassland | 141 |
| Ramsons | Forest | 100 |
| Red Clover | Grassland | 125 |
| Red Goosefoot | Garden | 84 |
| Red Valerian | Coastal | 167 |
| Redcurrant/Blackcurrant | Forest | 119 |
| Rock Samphire | Coastal | 168 |
| Rosemary | Garden | 39 |
| Sea Beet | Coastal | 171 |
| Sea Lettuce | Seaweed | 187 |
| Sea Purslane | Coastal | 173 |
| Smooth Sow Thistle | Grassland | 132 |
| Wall Pennywort | Garden | 40 |
| Watercress | Wetlands | 154 |
| Wild Basil | Grassland | 137 |
| Wild Cherry | Forest | 116 |
| Wild Marjoram | Grassland | 135 |
| Wild Raspberry | Forest | 117 |
| Wild Strawberry | Hedge | 73 |
| Wild Thyme | Garden | 136 |
| Woodruff | Forest | 112 |
| Yarrow | Grassland | 133 |

## Autumn

The autumn (September to November) can be a melancholic season with the first gales and rainstorms being in stark contrast to the warmth of the summer. However, for the forager it will be a busy time as the profusion of nuts and fruits must be gathered before they go rotten or are taken by the birds and squirrels (and other foragers!). This is the season of conserves with many kitchens smelling sweet from the pans of boiling fruit and sugar. Hard work in the autumn will be repaid with a larder full of jams, flavoured spirits and other delights which may either be eaten at leisure or given away as Christmas presents.

| Plant Name | Chapter | Page No. |
|---|---|---|
| Ash | Forest | 92 |
| Beech | Forest | 95 |
| Bilberry | Grassland | 121 |
| Biting Stonecrop | Garden | 45 |
| Black Mustard | Coastal | 161 |
| Blackberry | Hedge | 81 |
| Blackthorn (sloes) | Hedge | 55 |
| Chestnut, Sweet | Forest | 96 |
| Chickweed | Garden | 33 |
| Corn Salad | Grassland | 127 |
| Cowberry | Grassland | 139 |
| Crab Apple | Forest | 97 |
| Cranberry | Wetlands | 157 |
| Crowberry | Grassland | 140 |
| Dandelion | Garden | 36 |
| Elder | Forest | 101 |
| Fennel | Coastal | 163 |
| Hairy Bittercress | Garden | 41 |
| Hawthorn | Hedge | 64 |
| Hazel | Forest | 104 |
| Heather | Grassland | 129 |
| Juniper | Forest | 107 |
| Oak | Forest | 109 |
| Poppy | Grassland | 141 |
| Rape | Hedge | 161 |
| Red Clover | Grassland | 125 |
| Redcurrant/Blackcurrant | Forest | 119 |
| Rosemary | Garden | 39 |

| | | |
|---|---|---|
| Rowan | Forest | 108 |
| Sea Carrot/Wild Carrot | Coastal | 177 |
| Sea Purslane | Coastal | 173 |
| Silverweed | Hedge | 89 |
| Watercress | Wetlands | 154 |
| Wild Basil | Grassland | 137 |
| Wild Cherry | Forest | 116 |
| Wild Marjoram | Grassland | 135 |
| Wild Raspberry | Forest | 117 |

*Chapter Nine*

# A Summary of Plants

The following table offers a summary of the information offered in the main part of this book and should allow the reader to see the attributes of an individual plant at a glance. It is, however, recommended that the reader also consult individual plant entries as there may be advice/warnings relating to the picking and preparation of some species.

*A refreshing cup of herbal tea.*

| **Plant Name** | | **Book Entry** | | **Season** | | | | **Edible Part of the Plant** | | | | |
|---|---|---|---|---|---|---|---|---|---|---|---|---|
| *Common Name* | *Species Name* | *Chapter* | *Page No.* | *Winter* | *Spring* | *Summer* | *Autumn* | *Leaves* | *Shoots/ Stems* | *Flowers* | *Fruit/ Seed* | *Root/ Bulb* |
| Borage | *Borago officinalis* | Garden | 39 | | Y | Y | | Y | | Y | | |
| Burdock | *Arctium lappa* | Garden | 31 | | Y | Y | | Y | | | | Y |
| Chickweed | *Stellaria media* | Garden | 33 | Y | Y | Y | Y | Y | | Y | | |
| Coltsfoot | *Tussilago farfara* | Garden | 34 | | Y | | | | | Y | | |
| Dandelion | *Taraxacum officinale* | Garden | 36 | Y | Y | Y | Y | Y | | Y | | Y |
| Stinging Nettles | *Urtica dioica* | Garden | 49 | | Y | | | Y | | | | |
| Ground Elder | *Aegopodium podagraria* | Garden | 37 | | Y | | | Y | Y | | | |
| Rosemary | *Rosmarinus officinalis* | Garden | 39 | Y | Y | Y | Y | Y | | | | |
| Wall Pennywort | *Umbilicus rupestris* | Garden | 40 | | Y | Y | | Y | | | | |
| Hairy Bittercress | *Cardamine hirsuta* | Garden | 41 | | Y | Y | Y | Y | | | | |
| Ivy-Leaved Toadflax | *Cymbalaria muralis* | Garden | 43 | | Y | Y | | | | | | |
| Red Dead Nettle | *Lamium purpureum* | Garden | 48 | | Y | | | Y | | | | |
| White Dead Nettle | *Lamium album* | Garden | 48 | | Y | | | Y | | | | |
| Plantain, Greater | *Plantago major* | Garden | 44 | | Y | Y | | Y | | | | |
| Biting Stonecrop | *Sedum acre* | Garden | 45 | Y | Y | Y | Y | Y | | | | |
| Rosebay Willow-Herb | *Chamerion angustifolium* | Garden | 47 | | Y | | | Y | Y | | | |
| Lime Tree | *Tilia x europaea* | Garden | 52 | | Y | | | | | Y | | |
| Agrimony | *Agrimonia eupatoria* | Hedge | 53 | | | Y | | Y | | Y | | |
| Blackthorn (sloes) | *Prunus spinosa* | Hedge | 55 | Y | | | Y | | | | Y | |
| Cleavers | *Galium aparine* | Hedge | 57 | | Y | Y | | Y | | | | |

**Potential Culinary Uses**

| *Herb* | *Salads/ Raw* | *Garnish* | *Soups* | *Pasta/ Risotto* | *Vegetable* | *Conserve* | *Ingredient* | *Fermentation* | *Infusion* |
|---|---|---|---|---|---|---|---|---|---|
| Y | Y | Y | Y | Y | | | | | |
| | Y | | | | | | Y | | |
| | Y | | | Y | | | | | |
| | | | | | | | | Y | |
| | Y | Y | | | | | | | Y |
| | | | | | Y | | | | |
| Y | | | | | | | | | Y |
| | Y | Y | | | | | | | |
| | Y | Y | | | | | | | |
| | Y | Y | Y | | | | | | |
| | Y | Y | Y | | | | | | |
| | | | | | Y | | | | Y |
| | Y | Y | | | | | | | |
| | | | | | Y | | | | |
| | | | | | | | | | Y |
| | | | | | | | | | Y |
| | | | | | | Y | | | Y |
| | | | | | | | | | Y |

| **Plant Name** | | **Book Entry** | | **Season** | | | | **Edible Part of the Plant** | | | | |
|---|---|---|---|---|---|---|---|---|---|---|---|---|
| *Common Name* | *Species Name* | *Chapter* | *Page No.* | *Winter* | *Spring* | *Summer* | *Autumn* | *Leaves* | *Shoots/ Stems* | *Flowers* | *Fruit/ Seed* | *Root/ Bulb* |
| Sorrel, Common | *Rumex acetosa* | Hedge | 60 | | Y | | | Y | | | | |
| Garlic Mustard | *Alliaria petiolata* | Hedge | 61 | | Y | Y | | Y | | | | |
| Ground Ivy | *Glechoma hederacea* | Hedge | 63 | | Y | Y | | Y | Y | | | |
| Hawthorn | *Crataegus monogyna* | Hedge | 64 | | | | Y | | | Y | Y | |
| Horseradish | *Armoracia rusticana* | Hedge | 66 | Y | | | | | | | | Y |
| Primrose | *Primula vulgaris* | Hedge | 68 | | Y | | | Y | | Y | | |
| Tansy | *Tanacetum vulgare* | Hedge | 69 | | Y | | | Y | | | | |
| Hops, Wild | *Humulus lupulus* | Hedge | 71 | | Y | | | | | Y | | |
| Strawberry, Wild | *Fragaria vesca* | Hedge | 73 | | | Y | | | | | Y | |
| Wintercress | *Barbarea vulgaris* | Hedge | 75 | Y | Y | | | Y | | | | |
| Cow Parsley | *Anthriscus sylvestris* | Hedge | 76 | | Y | | | Y | | Y | | |
| Three-Cornered Garlic | *Allium triquetrum* | Hedge | 77 | | Y | | | Y | | | | |
| Bistort | *Persicaria bistorta* | Hedge | 80 | | Y | | | Y | Y | | | |
| Sweet Cicely | *Myrrhis odorata* | Hedge | 79 | | Y | | | Y | | Y | | |
| Blackberry | *Rubus fructicosus* | Hedge | 81 | | | | Y | | | | Y | |
| Good King Henry | *Chenopodium bonus-henricus* | Hedge | 83 | | Y | Y | | Y | Y | | | |
| Fat Hen | *Chenopodium album* | Hedge | 84 | | Y | Y | | Y | Y | | | |
| Mugwort | *Artemisia vulgaris* | Hedge | 85 | | Y | Y | | Y | | | | |
| Silverweed | *Argentina anserine* | Hedge | 89 | | Y | | Y | Y | | | | Y |
| Medlar | *Mespilus germanica* | Hedge | 88 | Y | | | | | | | Y | |

| Potential Culinary Uses | | | | | | | | | |
|---|---|---|---|---|---|---|---|---|---|
| *Herb* | *Salads/ Raw* | *Garnish* | *Soups* | *Pasta/ Risotto* | *Vegetable* | *Conserve* | *Ingredient* | *Fermentation* | *Infusion* |
| | Y | Y | Y | Y | | | | | |
| | Y | | Y | | Y | | | | |
| | | | | | | | | | Y |
| | | | | | | Y | | | Y |
| | | | | | | Y | | | |
| | | | | | | | | | |
| | | | | | | | Y | | |
| | | | | | Y | | Y | Y | |
| | Y | | | | | Y | Y | | |
| | Y | | | Y | Y | | | | |
| | | Y | | | | | | | Y |
| | | Y | Y | Y | | | | | |
| | | | Y | | Y | | Y | | |
| Y | Y | | Y | Y | Y | | | | Y |
| | Y | | | | | Y | Y | Y | |
| | | | | Y | Y | | | | |
| | | | | | Y | | | | |
| Y | | | | | | | | | Y |
| | | | | | Y | | | | Y |
| | | | | | | Y | | | |

| **Plant Name** | | **Book Entry** | | **Season** | | | | **Edible Part of the Plant** | | | | |
|---|---|---|---|---|---|---|---|---|---|---|---|---|
| *Common Name* | *Species Name* | *Chapter* | *Page No.* | *Winter* | *Spring* | *Summer* | *Autumn* | *Leaves* | *Shoots/ Stems* | *Flowers* | *Fruit/ Seed* | *Root/ Bulb* |
| Ash | *Fraxinus excelsior* | Forest | 92 | | | | Y | | | | Y | |
| Beech | *Fagus sylvatica* | Forest | 95 | | | | Y | | | | Y | |
| Chestnut, Sweet | *Castanea sativa* | Forest | 96 | | | | Y | | | | Y | |
| Crab Apple | *Malus sylvestris* | Forest | 97 | | | | Y | | | | Y | |
| Elder Tree | *Sambucus nigra* | Forest | 101 | | Y | | Y | | | Y | Y | |
| Hazel Tree | *Corylus avellana* | Forest | 104 | | | | Y | | | | Y | |
| Wood Avens | *Geum urbanum* | Forest | 105 | | Y | | | | | | | Y |
| Juniper | *Juniperus communis* | Forest | 107 | | | | Y | | | | Y | |
| Rowan | *Sorbus aucuparia* | Forest | 108 | | | | Y | | | | Y | |
| Oak Tree, English | *Quercus rober* | Forest | 109 | | | | Y | | | | Y | |
| Pignut | *Conopodium majus* | Forest | 111 | | Y | | | | | | | Y |
| Ramsons | *Allium ursinum* | Forest | 100 | | Y | Y | | Y | | | | |
| Woodruff, Sweet | *Galium odoratum* | Forest | 112 | | Y | Y | | Y | Y | Y | | |
| Hogweed, Common | *Heracleum sphondylium* | Forest | 113 | | Y | Y | | | Y | | | |
| Broom, Common | *Cytisus scoparius* | Forest | 115 | | Y | | | | | Y | | |
| Cherry, Wild | Prunus avium | Forest | 116 | | | Y | Y | | | | Y | |
| Raspberry, Wild | *Rubus idaeus* | Forest | 117 | | | Y | Y | | | | Y | |
| Black Currant | *Ribes nigrum* | Forest | 119 | | | Y | Y | | | | Y | |
| Red Currant | *Ribes rubrum* | Forest | 119 | | | Y | Y | | | | Y | |
| Bilberry | *Vaccinium myrtillus* | Grassland | 121 | | | Y | Y | | | | | |

| Potential Culinary Uses | | | | | | | | | |
|---|---|---|---|---|---|---|---|---|---|
| *Herb* | *Salads/ Raw* | *Garnish* | *Soups* | *Pasta/ Risotto* | *Vegetable* | *Conserve* | *Ingredient* | *Fermentation* | *Infusion* |
| | | | | | | Y | | | Y |
| | Y | | | | | Y | | | |
| | | | | | Y | Y | Y | | |
| | | | | | | Y | Y | Y | |
| | | | | | | Y | Y | Y | Y |
| | Y | Y | | | | | Y | | |
| Y | | | | | | | | | |
| | | | | | | | Y | | |
| | | | | | | Y | | Y | |
| | | | | | | | | | Y |
| | Y | | Y | | | | | | |
| | Y | Y | | Y | | | | | |
| | | | | | | | | | Y |
| | | | | Y | Y | | | | |
| | Y | | | | | | | Y | |
| | Y | | | | | Y | Y | Y | |
| | Y | | | | | Y | Y | Y | |
| | Y | | | | | Y | Y | Y | |
| | Y | | | | | Y | Y | Y | |

| **Plant Name** | | **Book Entry** | | **Season** | | | | **Edible Part of the Plant** | | | | |
|---|---|---|---|---|---|---|---|---|---|---|---|---|
| *Common Name* | *Species Name* | *Chapter* | *Page No.* | *Winter* | *Spring* | *Summer* | *Autumn* | *Leaves* | *Shoots/ Stems* | *Flowers* | *Fruit/ Seed* | *Root/ Bulb* |
| Chamomile | *Anthemis nobilis* | Grassland | 124 | | Y | Y | | | | | | |
| Red Clover | *Trifolium praetense* | Grassland | 125 | | | Y | Y | | | | | |
| Corn Salad | *Valerianella locusta* | Grassland | 127 | | Y | | Y | | | | | |
| Gorse, Common | *Ulex europaeus* | Grassland | 128 | | Y | | | | | | | |
| Heather | *Calluna vulgaris* | Grassland | 129 | | | Y | Y | | | Y | | |
| Salad Burnet | *Sanguisorba minor* | Grassland | 131 | | Y | | | Y | | | | |
| Sow Thistle | *Sonchus oleraceus* | Grassland | 132 | | Y | Y | | Y | | | | |
| Yarrow | *Achillea millefolium* | Grassland | 133 | | Y | Y | | Y | | | | |
| Marjoram, Wild | *Origanum vulgare* | Grassland | 135 | | Y | Y | Y | Y | | | | |
| Thyme, Wild | *Thymus polytrichus* | Grassland | 136 | | | Y | | Y | | Y | | |
| Basil, Wild | *Clinopodium vulgare* | Grassland | 137 | | Y | Y | Y | Y | | | | |
| Cowberry | *Vaccinium vitis-idaea* | Grassland | 139 | | | | Y | | | | Y | |
| Crowberry | *Empetrum nigrum* | Grassland | 140 | Y | | | Y | | | | Y | |
| Poppy, Common | *Papaver rhoeas* | Grassland | 141 | | | Y | Y | | | | Y | |
| Parsnips, Wild | *Pastinaca sativa* | Grassland | 147 | Y | | | | | | | | Y |
| Mint | *Mentha spp.* | Grassland | 144 | | | | | Y | | | | |
| Catmint/ catnip | *Nepeta cataria* | Grassland | 145 | | Y | Y | | Y | Y | | | |
| Bog Myrtle | *Myrica gale* | Wetlands | 151 | | | Y | | Y | | | | |
| Lady's Smock | *Cardamine pratensis* | Wetlands | 152 | | Y | | | Y | | | | |
| Meadowsweet | *Filipendula ulmaria* | Wetlands | 153 | | Y | Y | | Y | | Y | | |
| Watercress | *Rorippa nasturtium-aquaticum* | Wetlands | 154 | Y | Y | Y | Y | Y | | | | |

**Potential Culinary Uses**

| *Herb* | *Salads/ Raw* | *Garnish* | *Soups* | *Pasta/ Risotto* | *Vegetable* | *Conserve* | *Ingredient* | *Fermentation* | *Infusion* |
|---|---|---|---|---|---|---|---|---|---|
| | | | | | | | | Y | Y |
| | Y | | | | | | | Y | |
| | Y | | | | | | | | |
| | | | | | | | | | Y |
| Y | | | | | | | | | |
| Y | | Y | Y | Y | | | | | Y |
| Y | Y | | Y | Y | | | | | |
| | | | | | | Y | | | |
| | | | | | | Y | | | |
| | | Y | | | | | Y | | |
| | | | Y | | Y | | | | |
| Y | | Y | | | | Y | | | Y |
| Y | | | | | | | | | |
| | | | | | | | | Y | |
| | Y | Y | | | | | | | |
| | | | | | | | | Y | |
| | Y | Y | Y | | | | | | |

| Plant Name | | Book Entry | | Season | | | | Edible Part of the Plant | | | | |
|---|---|---|---|---|---|---|---|---|---|---|---|---|
| *Common Name* | *Species Name* | *Chapter* | *Page No.* | *Winter* | *Spring* | *Summer* | *Autumn* | *Leaves* | *Shoots/ Stems* | *Flowers* | *Fruit/ Seed* | *Root/ Bulb* |
| Comfrey | *Symphytum officinale* | Wetlands | 156 | | Y | | | Y | | | | |
| Cranberry, European | *Vaccinium oxycoccus* | Wetlands | 157 | | | Y | Y | | | | Y | |
| Alexanders | *Smyrnium olusatrum* | Coastal | 160 | | Y | | | | Y | | | |
| Black Mustard | *Brassica nigra* | Coastal | 161 | | Y | | Y | Y | | | Y | |
| Fennel | *Foeniculum vulgare* | Coastal | 163 | | | Y | Y | Y | Y | Y | | Y |
| Mallow, Common | *Malva sylvestris* | Coastal | 164 | | Y | | | Y | | | | |
| Marsh Samphire | *Salicornica europaea* | Coastal | 165 | | Y | Y | | | Y | | | |
| Red Valerian | *Centranthus ruber* | Coastal | 167 | | Y | Y | | Y | | | | Y |
| Rock Samphire | *Crithmumm-aritimum* | Coastal | 168 | | Y | Y | | Y | | | | |
| Scurvy Grass | *Cochlearia officinalis* | Coastal | 169 | | Y | | | Y | | | | |
| Sea Beet | *Beta vulgaris subsp. maritima* | Coastal | 171 | | Y | Y | | Y | | | | |
| Sea Kale | *Crambe maritima* | Coastal | 172 | | Y | | | | Y | | | |
| Sea Purslane | *Atriplex portulacoides* | Coastal | 173 | Y | Y | Y | Y | Y | | | | |
| Cabbage, Wild | *Brassic oleracea* | Coastal | 175 | | Y | | | Y | | | | |
| Carrot, Wild/ Sea Carrot | *Daucus carota* | Coastal | 177 | | | | Y | | | | | Y |
| Carragheen | *Chondrus crispus* | Seaweed | 181 | | Y | Y | | Y | | | | |
| Laver | *Porphyra umbilicalis* | Seaweed | 183 | | Y | Y | | Y | | | | |
| Dulse | *Palmaria palmata* | Seaweed | 185 | | Y | Y | | Y | | | | |
| Sea Lettuce | *Ulva lactuca* | Seaweed | 187 | | Y | Y | | Y | | | | |

| Potential Culinary Uses | | | | | | | | | |
|---|---|---|---|---|---|---|---|---|---|
| *Herb* | *Salads/ Raw* | *Garnish* | *Soups* | *Pasta/ Risotto* | *Vegetable* | *Conserve* | *Ingredient* | *Fermentation* | *Infusion* |
| | | | | | | | | Y | Y |
| | Y | | | | | | | Y | |
| | Y | | | | | | | | |
| | | | | | | | | | Y |
| Y | | | | | | | | | |
| Y | | Y | Y | Y | | | | | Y |
| Y | Y | | Y | Y | | | | | |
| | | | | | | Y | | | |
| | | | | | | Y | | | |
| | | Y | | | | | Y | | |
| | | | Y | | Y | | | | |
| Y | | Y | | | | Y | | | Y |
| Y | | | | | | | | | |
| | | | | | | | | Y | |
| | Y | Y | | | | | | | |
| | | | | | | | | Y | |
| | Y | Y | Y | | | | | | |

| **Plant Name** | | **Book Entry** | | **Season** | | | | **Edible Part of the Plant** | | | | |
|---|---|---|---|---|---|---|---|---|---|---|---|---|
| *Common Name* | *Species Name* | *Chapter* | *Page No.* | *Winter* | *Spring* | *Summer* | *Autumn* | *Leaves* | *Shoots/ Stems* | *Flowers* | *Fruit/ Seed* | *Root/ Bulb* |
| Comfrey | *Symphytum officinale* | Wetlands | 156 | | Y | | | Y | | | | |
| Cranberry, European | *Vaccinium oxycoccus* | Wetlands | 157 | | | Y | Y | | | | Y | |
| Alexanders | *Smyrnium olusatrum* | Coastal | 160 | | Y | | | | Y | | | |
| Black Mustard | *Brassica nigra* | Coastal | 161 | | Y | | Y | Y | | | Y | |
| Fennel | *Foeniculum vulgare* | Coastal | 163 | | | Y | Y | Y | Y | Y | | Y |
| Mallow, Common | *Malva sylvestris* | Coastal | 164 | | Y | | | Y | | | | |
| Marsh Samphire | *Salicornica europaea* | Coastal | 165 | | Y | Y | | | Y | | | |
| Red Valerian | *Centranthus ruber* | Coastal | 167 | | Y | Y | | Y | | | | Y |
| Rock Samphire | *Crithmumm-aritimum* | Coastal | 168 | | Y | Y | | Y | | | | |
| Scurvy Grass | *Cochlearia officinalis* | Coastal | 169 | | Y | | | Y | | | | |
| Sea Beet | *Beta vulgaris subsp. maritima* | Coastal | 171 | | Y | Y | | Y | | | | |
| Sea Kale | *Crambe maritima* | Coastal | 172 | | Y | | | | Y | | | |
| Sea Purslane | *Atriplex portulacoides* | Coastal | 173 | Y | Y | Y | Y | Y | | | | |
| Cabbage, Wild | *Brassic oleracea* | Coastal | 175 | | Y | | | Y | | | | |
| Carrot, Wild/ Sea Carrot | *Daucus carota* | Coastal | 177 | | | | Y | | | | | Y |
| Carragheen | *Chondrus crispus* | Seaweed | 181 | | Y | Y | | Y | | | | |
| Laver | *Porphyra umbilicalis* | Seaweed | 183 | | Y | Y | | Y | | | | |
| Dulse | *Palmaria palmata* | Seaweed | 185 | | Y | Y | | Y | | | | |
| Sea Lettuce | *Ulva lactuca* | Seaweed | 187 | | Y | Y | | Y | | | | |

| Potential Culinary Uses | | | | | | | | | |
|---|---|---|---|---|---|---|---|---|---|
| *Herb* | *Salads/ Raw* | *Garnish* | *Soups* | *Pasta/ Risotto* | *Vegetable* | *Conserve* | *Ingredient* | *Fermentation* | *Infusion* |
| | | | Y | Y | | | | | |
| | | | | | | Y | | | |
| | | | Y | Y | Y | | | | |
| Y | Y | | | | Y | | | | |
| | | | Y | | Y | | | | |
| | | | | | Y | | | | |
| | | | | | Y | Y | | | |
| | Y | | Y | | | | | | |
| | Y | | Y | Y | Y | | | | |
| | Y | Y | | | | | | | |
| | | | | | Y | | Y | | |
| | | | | | Y | | | | |
| | | | | | Y | | | | |
| | | | | | Y | | Y | | |
| | | | Y | | Y | | | | |
| | | | Y | | | | Y | | |
| | | | Y | | Y | | Y | | |
| | Y | | Y | | Y | | Y | | |
| | Y | | Y | | Y | | Y | | |

# Bibliography


Barton, B., 1837. *The British Flora Medica*. London: Woodfall & Co.

Baylis, E., 1791. *A New and Compleat Body of Practical Botanic Physic*. London: Stace & Maids.

Beauvilliers, A., 1827. *The Art of French Cookery*. London: Longman & Co.

Boerhaave, H., 1715. *Boerhaave's Aphorisms: Concerning the Knowledge and Cure of Diseases*. London: Cowse and Innys.

Briggs, R., 1788. *The English Art of Cookery*. London: J. Robinson.

Chambers, R., 1832. *The Book of Days*. London: R. Chambers.

Claudius, J., 1838. *Arboretum et Fruticetum Britannicum*. London: Longman & Co.

Collingwood, F., 1792. *The Universal Cook, and City and Country Housekeeper*. London: Scratchead and Letterman.

Culpeper, N., 1770. *The English Physician*. London: Ballard & Co. (Originally published in 1652.)

Eastoe, J., 2008. *Wild Food*. London: Anova.

Eaton, M., 1822. *The Cook and Housekeeper's Complete and Universal Dictionary*. Suffolk: Bungay.

Ellis, W., 1749. *A Compleat System of Experienced Improvements, made on Sheep*. London: Astley.

Fletcher, N., 2007. *The Easy Wild Food Guide*. London: Aurum Press.

Frazer, M., 1820. *The Practice of Cookery, Pastry, and Confectionary*. Edinburgh: Mrs Frazer.

Gerard, J., 1633. *Great Herball, or Generall Historie of Plantes*. London: J. Gerard. (Originally published in 1597.)

Gray, S., 1821. *A Natural Arrangement of British Plants*. London: Baldwin, Craddock & Joy.

Harrison, S., 1739. *The House Keeper's Pocket Book*. London: Ware.

Hill, J., 1812. *The Family Herbal*. London: Brightly & Co.

Hilton, J., 2007. *Wild Food for Free*. London: Gaia Books.

Holland, M., 1837. *The Complete Economical Cook, and Frugal Housewife*. London: T. Tegg & Son.

Hooker, W., 1821. *Flora Scotia*. London: Archibald Constable & Co.

Lee, K., 1832. *The Cook's Own Book*. Boston: Monroe & Francis.

Leslie, E., 1832. *Seventy-five Receipts for Pastry, Cakes and Sweetmeats.* Boston: Monroe & Francis.
Link, H., 1822. *Elementa Philosophiae Botanicae*. London: Clowes & Co.
Low, D., 1834. *Elements of Practical Agriculture*. Edinburgh: Bell and Bradfute.
Mabey, R., 2001. *Food for Free*. London: HarperCollins.
MacArtain, P., Gill, C., Brooks, M., Campbell, R., & Rowland, I., 2007, 'Nutritional Value of Edible Seaweeds', *Nutrition Reviews*, Vol. 65(12), pp. 535–543.
Mackay, J., 1836. *Flora Hibernica*. London: Curry & Co.
Markham, G., 1668. *A Way to Get Wealth*. London: John Streater.
Michael, P., 2007. *Edible Wild Plants and Herbs*. London: Grub Street.
Miller, P., 1835. *The Gardener's Dictionary*. London: G. Henderson.
Mudie, R., 1837. *Spring*. London: Thomas Ward & Co.
Murray, J., 1808. *Elements of Materia Medica and Pharmacy*. Philadelphia: Kite & Co.
Nisbet, W., 1801. *A Practical Treatise on Diet*. London: R. Philips.
Northcote, J., & Harvey, W., 1829. *One Hundred Fables, Original and Selected*. London: G. Lawford.
Petiver, J., 1714. *Mr. Petiver's English Herbal*. London: J. Petiver.
Petiver, J., 1717. *Plantæ Silesiacæ Rariores ac Desideratæ*. London: J. Petiver.
Philips, H., 1829. *Flora Historica*. London: Lloyd & Son.
Phillips, R., 1983. *Wild Food*. London: Macmillan.
Pinkerton, J., 1811. *A General Collection of the Best and Most Interesting Voyages and Travels*. London: Longman & Co.
Ray, J., & Petiver, J. *Herbarii Britannici*. London: J. Petiver.
Rogers, J., 1843. *The Vegetable Cultivator*. London: Longman & Co.
Rundell, E., 1826. *New System of Domestic Cookery*. London: J. Murray.
Salisbury, W., 1816. *The Botanist's Companion*. London: Longman & Co.
Sinclair, G., 1826. *Hortus Gramineus Woburnensis*. London: J. Ridgway.
Smith, J., 1803. *The English Flora*. London: Longman & Co.
Smith, J. & Sowerby, J., 1790–1813. *English Botany*. London: J. Davis.
Spratt, G., 1829. *Flora Medica*. London: Callow & Wilson.
Thornton, J., 1814. *New Family Herbal*. London: Richard Phillips.
Verral, W., 1759. *A Complete System of Cookery*. London: Verral.
Woodville, W., 1832. *Medical Botany*. London: J. Bohn.

# Acknowledgements

Putting this book together has been great fun and I am grateful to the many people who have been kind enough to share their expertise and advice with me. Some people have asked to remain anonymous but I would particularly like to thank Jim Davy, John and Elizabeth Baxter, Karl Hairon, Tim le Gallais, Theresa Coombs and Adrian Hunt.

I would like to thank the staff at the following institutions for allowing me access to their records and for their patience when answering my many questions: British Library; British Newspaper Library; Cambridge University Library; The National Archives; Institute of Historical Research; Natural History Museum; Royal Historical Society; Société Jersiaise, University College London and Wellcome Institute Library.

A big thank-you must go to the staff at Pen and Sword and especially Fiona Shoop, Lisa Hooson and Pamela Covey whose support and enthusiasm for this project ensured that the production process went without a hitch. I would like to thank my wonderful agent Mandy Little (of Waston, Little) for her continued guidance. Finally, this project could not have been undertaken without the support of my immediate and extended family and especially my father, Martyn Chambers, and my parents-in-law, John and Elizabeth Baxter. My greatest debt is to my wife Rachel and daughter Eleanor whose sense of humour and patience is apparently without limit. I love you both, always and forever.